THE VERSATILE SALESPERSON

Selling the Way Your Customer Wants to Buy

D0823205

THE VERSATILE SALESPERSON

Selling the Way Your Customer Wants to Buy

Roger Wenschlag

Wilson Learning Corporation

edited by

Sharyn Skeeter

WILEY

John Wiley & Sons, Inc.

New York • Chichester • Brisbane • Toronto • Singapore

Publisher: Stephen Kippur
Editor: David Sobel
Managing Editor: Ruth Greif
Editing, Design, and Production: Publications Development Company

This publication is designed to provide accurate and authoritative
information in regard to the subject matter covered. It is sold with
the understanding that the publisher is not engaged in rendering
professional advice. If professional advice or other expert assistance
is required, the services of a competent professional person should
be sought.

Copyright © 1987, 1989 by John Wiley & Sons, Inc.

All rights reserved. Published simultaneously in Canada.

Reproduction or translation of any part of this work beyond
that permitted by Section 107 or 108 of the 1976
United States Copyright Act without the permission of
the copyright owner is unlawful. Requests for permission
or further information should be addressed to the
Permissions Department, John Wiley & Sons, Inc.

Library of Congress Cataloging-in-Publication Data

Wenschlag, Roger.
  The versatile salesperson.

  Includes index.
  1. Selling. I. Title.
HF5438.25.W294   1987   658.8'5   87-2003
ISBN 0-471-85436-0
ISBN 0-471-50379-7 (pbk.)
Printed in the United States of America

89 90 10 9 8 7 6 5 4 3 2 1

Contents

Foreword

The job of a professional salesperson is as complex as it is interesting and rewarding. Selling requires mastery of a broad range of skills and knowledge. Selling skills, product/service knowledge, business and industry knowledge, and self-development all contribute to the effectiveness of the salesperson.

This book is about selling skills—specifically the skill of sales versatility, your ability to develop and maintain your buyers' comfort throughout the sales process. In other words, to sell the way your buyers like to buy.

Versatility can help you in a number of ways. Through it you can

1. Achieve more positive call outcomes,
2. Convert more prospects to buyers,
3. Increase your sales,
4. Develop more long-term business relationships, and
5. Reduce your own tension in uncomfortable relationships.

Versatility means having the ability to positively develop interpersonal relationships with your buyers. The salesperson without versatility skills is almost certain to find it more difficult to be successful. Consider a few of the realities of the marketplace:

- Product exclusivity is short-lived.
- Buyers perceive little differentiation between suppliers and vendors.

- Manufacturers adopt the commodity approach, seeking only to become the most cost-effective producer in their market segment.
- Price remains a factor in the buying decision, and buyers always want value and quality within their economic constraints.
- Today's market is buyer-oriented.

People buy, they are not sold! You can get ahead only by earning buyer trust, by building positive interpersonal relationships with potential buyers, and by strengthening relationships with existing buyers. Versatility is a valuable tool for cultivating all of these.

To facilitate the reading of this book, we have used the generic "he" rather than such awkward constructions as "he or she" or "he/she." No slight is intended; our only desire is to provide the highest level of clarity in the writing of this book.

This book provides insights and practical ideas about versatility in three ways: (1) you will learn how to identify the social style of your buyers, (2) you will learn the selling preferences and expectations of the four social styles, and (3) you will learn specific ways to modify your selling behavior and practice selling strategies that will make your buyer most comfortable with you.

With time and effort you can become very adept at sales versatility. In doing so, the payoff for both you and your buyer will be substantial.

ROGER WENSCHLAG
Wilson Learning Corporation

1

Versatility: The Key to Competence in Selling

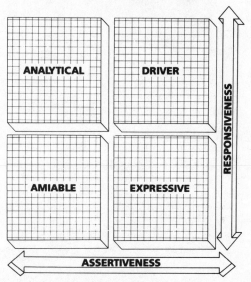

"In direct sales, purchases are made emotionally. When I made standard presentations, sometimes I would be on a streak. I felt that there would be no way I could miss. That is, until the next time—when I wouldn't be able to close the sale. You could say, I had many ups and downs," says Wayne Provart of his early days selling training materials.

Wayne discovered that what got a sale with one customer, would hardly get a foot in the door with another. His standard presentations lacked the versatility that is necessary for adapting to the needs of different buyers. How would this have helped him? Well, let us first take a look at what versatility is.

Versatility is the degree to which a salesperson is perceived as developing and maintaining buyer comfort throughout the sales process.

That means that versatility in sales reflects your ability to adapt your behavior to make your buyer most comfortable with you and the sales situation. Why is this important? The realities of today's marketplace make it so. Here are just a few reasons.

- *Today's marketplace is buyer-oriented.* Your customers buy, they are not sold.
- *Buyers perceive little differentiation between suppliers and vendors.* It's up to you to build a relationship so that the buyer can see a difference.
- *Price remains a factor in the buying decision, but buyers always want value and quality within their economic constraints.* You give them the reason for trusting your product's quality.

- *Product exclusivity is short-lived.* You cannot expect to corner the market forever.
- *Manufacturers adopt the commodity approach, seeking only to become the most cost-effective producer in their market.* To counter this, you have to show the buyer how your product, rather than your competitor's product, is better suited to your buyer's needs.

Let's use these points in looking at a successful sale.

Jeff Holte, about thirty, is a salesman from Clark-Data. He is calling on Garth Stapels, the vice president of MIS for a large urban bank. Garth, in his early forties, is neatly dressed. His high-tech office is well organized. Both Jeff and Garth seem a bit cautious when they shake hands and Jeff offers Garth his card.

Garth says tentatively, "Well, now let's see . . . I got the information you sent me."

"Good. Did Jane Gilbert speak to you?"

"Yes. Yes she did. She was the one who recommended your automatic teller machine system."

"Well, that's good to hear. Jane Gilbert and I met last week. She was able to detail some of your plans for the future."

"Then you know we're thinking about replacements."

When Jeff responds, "Yes," Garth realizes that it's time to get down to business. "Oh, please, sit down. I'm afraid I've only got about half an hour."

Jeff begins his presentation by setting up a three-ring binder-sized flip chart featuring graphics, figures, and other material. He has his calculator ready on the desk. Using his flip chart for illustration, he starts giving background information on Clark-Data. He ends this introduction with, "They were convinced, and time has proven them right, that durability was going to be as big a criterion as function for the informed buyer."

Garth, who has been listening attentively, responds, "That's easy to envision, but hard to deliver. How does your unit handle on-line failures?"

"Good question. Brings me to my next point, the actual design of the stand-alone CPU." Jeff explains, then sums up with, "so, while a traditional system has eight critical variables that can routinely cause failures, the Clark has two."

Garth checks this on his calculator. "Oh, I see where you're going. Okay, well let's say then that each machine in a twenty-machine network makes 8000 transactions a month."

Jeff adds, "OK. And let's say you have an eight variable system with each variable having a mean failure rate of 5 percent . . ." and finishes the calculation.

Garth checks the numbers. "Well, that's important, and too often overlooked. But to be fair, let's apply the same criteria to your machine's Mean-Time-Between-Failure rate."

Jeff flips to a page on his display, "I have that information right here."

They both smile when Garth says, "Somehow I just knew you'd have the figures." He's pleased with the facts. "Well, that has a significant impact on the reliability, and the bottom line."

"This is good information. Listen, before we go on any further, I want to call Jane Gilbert and have her join us. She's done a very detailed analysis of our needs. I think this is precisely the kind of information she's looking for."

Jeff Holte kept to his standard presentation—and it worked perfectly with Garth. It is likely that he will succeed and their relationship will continue. Why was Jeff able to make this sale? He was neat, businesslike, organized. He seemed to understand Garth's needs and he had all the facts to back up his claims about Clark-Data. This was just what Garth wanted.

Try listing some of your own sales experiences where the buyer liked your approach. What did you do that made the buyer comfortable? Why did it seem to work so well for this buyer?

Now, let's take a look at Jeff Holte on a different sales call. This time he is calling on Hal MacFarland.

Hal, in his forties, is vice president of operations of an urban bank. Before Jeff arrives, Hal is standing with his back to his desk, cheerfully setting up a tennis match with a friend on the phone, and practicing his forehand with an imaginary tennis racket. His athletic bag and racket are on his desk with his computer terminal and a few files. When his secretary announces Jeff Holte's arrival, Hal ends his phone call, hides his tennis racket and bag, quickly puts on his suit jacket, and says, "Hi, you must be Jeff from Clark-Data?"

"Right. Jeff Holte." He hands Hal his card. "I'm glad to get this opportunity to meet you, Mr. MacFarland. I've heard a lot about you and your operation here."

"Hal. Just call me Hal. Yeah, Dorothy Griffin down in Data Processing has good things to say about you and Clark-Data."

"We met last week to talk about ATM options."

"Well, then you know that we're planning a big expansion of automated services."

"Right. And Clark-Data would like to be involved. Why don't I start by telling you a little bit about Clark-Data. Would that be all right?"

Hal, surprised by Jeff's formality, says, "Sure."

While presenting the background of the company with his flip chart, Jeff mentions, "The founders wanted to develop a truly reliable, highly advanced automated teller machine."

Hal interrupts, "Reliable is exactly what we need here. Say, did you see the article in the newspaper this morning about that money machine in Denver?"

"Uh, no."

"Seems it spewed out a few thousand dollars to a couple of guys. Wouldn't that be enough to spoil your day, especially if you're in charge of operations?"

"Right. That's been a minor problem with earlier machines. We've pretty much solved that with our line of RX-5s."

"Mother of pearl! If that had happened here, somebody would have taken the big dive." He gestures diving out the window.

Jeff, unresponsive to Hal's attempt at humor, finds a page in his flip chart to show Hal. "In fact, as you can see here, our data shows how that sort of incident has declined over the last ten years . . . that's this green line here . . . contrasted to bank acceptance—that's this blue line."

Hal, fidgeting, says, "Um hmm."

Jeff continues to page through his display and discuss background information about Clark-Data's experience in the automated teller business, ". . . so our CPU is directly linked to an internal fallback system that allows it to operate even if there is a failure somewhere else on the line."

"Well, that's certainly something to think about." Hal is trying to look interested.

"Now, let's compare a conventional on-line ATM against Clark's."

Hal interrupts. "Say, you know something, I think Bob Sharkey should hear this. C'mon, let's go down to his office. We'll grab a cup of coffee on the way." Hal moves toward the door and waits for Jeff to get his briefcase. "Yeah, that article was really something. I mean it wouldn't be so bad if you were on the receiving end . . . So, tell me more about customer acceptance. Do people really use your machine, or what?"

Jeff tries to flip through his display while walking down the hallway. "Ah, absolutely. In fact, these independent studies—let's see, where are these studies? See, these studies show that in the last five years customer acceptance has gone up 25 percent."

"But what does that mean in terms of cost-benefit to the bank?"

"Well, that's an important question . . ." Jeff takes out his calculator and begins to figure. Hal introduces Jeff to Sally Peterson from the Strategic Marketing department. Jeff looks up briefly to say "Hello" then goes back to his calculator. "According to my figures, if you installed fifteen of our machines you could expect approximately a 5 percent improvement in deposits by the second year. Well, that would basically pay for the units by the third year depending on your amortization schedule, of course."

"Of course. Say, let's grab that cup of coffee. How do you like it?"

"Black's fine."

"Well, at least you like your coffee uncomplicated!" Hal sees Howard Oates walking up to the coffee counter. "Howard, just the man I'm looking for. Jeff Holte, this is Howard Oates. He's with our Financial Analysis group. Jeff here works for Clark-Data. You know, they make Automated Teller Machines. Jeff, here's what I'm thinking. I'd like you to get together with Howard here, and give him your stuff, and then he and I can get together this afternoon sometime for a meeting. I want to give Bob Sharkey a call. And if he likes your stuff then we'll all get together for a meeting sometime, OK? So, Howard, give me a call around 4 about this."

After Hal leaves, Howard hesitantly says to Jeff, "So, a new line of ATM's? I don't know about this expansion plan. You know, our folks ran a cost analysis on this last month and it showed the cost-benefit line to be flat for about six years, especially when you add in the effects of inflation . . ."

What happened in this sales call? At first, Jeff might have had the chance to get the sale because Hal seemed to be interested in ATMs. Unfortunately, Jeff had trouble seeing Hal's needs and expectations. He didn't notice that Hal was not responding to his approach. The possibility of developing a positive sales relationship was lost and Hal probably won't buy.

In this case, Jeff used almost the same approach with Hal as he did, successfully, with Garth. What he didn't recognize was:

- Buyers differ and have different expectations of salespeople.
- Buyers give signals when their expectations are and aren't being met.
- Salespeople need to adapt their behavior to different buyers.

At the beginning of Jeff's sales calls, both Garth and Hal seemed like neutral prospects. At the end of the calls, Garth had become a likely sale, while Hal was an unlikely sale. With four out of ten prospects neutral or undecided, it certainly would be advantageous to convert as many of these prospects to likely sales as possible. By using different approaches, Jeff can make fewer high probability calls to make sales. All Jeff has to do is adapt his behavior to his potential buyers. (See Exhibit 1.)

WHAT DO DIFFERENT BUYERS EXPECT?

To get an idea of what buyers want, we asked four prospects, "As a buyer, what do you expect from a salesperson?"

Buyer 1. Well, I guess the most important thing is that you're honest and open with me. I always feel it's awkward when people have hidden agendas, don't you?

I am more receptive when salespeople are relaxed and able to show concern for me and my problems. I want that person to

SALES CONVERSION

Exhibit 1   Sales Conversion

For every 10 prospects we call on, probability says:
3 will be Likely Sales;
3 will be Unlikely Sales; and
4 will be Neutral/Undecided

talk to me about my company. I want to know we can work together.

Ask questions in detail. Information, and time to digest it, is important for both of us.

You know, most of us who buy for companies arrive at decisions in much the same way. It helps me, though, if you're honest, straightforward, and dependable. I want to know I'm working with an effective problem solver who has solid product knowledge. And most of all, give me assurance that what you're proposing will benefit me and my people.

You know, isn't sales essentially communication? People talking, getting things done.

Buyer 2. First of all, I would prefer to deal with you in a businesslike manner. That's not to say I wouldn't like to visit, but time is important. This organization doesn't run by itself. It's unique. Maintaining a competitive edge takes time and energy.

Second, I like someone who is thorough and precise, basically well-prepared and organized. I like getting it down on paper.

Third, I'm not interested in hearing a lot of wild claims, or half-baked ideas. Tangible, practical suggestions are what I need.

Finally, when we're finished, I'd like to have a clear plan of action, including follow-through. Too many salespeople fail to follow-through.

I think that covers everything.

Buyer 3. I like salespeople who are properly dressed, who step up to bat; who stick to the point.

Be prepared. That means you should know my situation before recommending what you've got. Ask questions, and then listen. Don't play the know-it-all. We've all met the guy who wanted to tell Noah about the flood.

Show me that you understand my problem, and then tell me what your product or service can do. But don't box me in. Give me options, choices.

Bring written information, something I can read.

Buyer 4. We have a fellow who comes in here . . . handles our employee benefit plan. He's what I expect in a salesperson. One of these days everyone is going to sell like Phil.

With Phil you get a strong feeling for the person you're dealing with. He understands me and my department.

I like salespeople who are decisive, but that doesn't mean we can't take time to toss ideas around. I like that, so don't pressure me into making a decision right off the bat.

Let me know you have the facts, but don't wear me out with every little detail. If you have information, great. Write it down.

I like salespeople who are competent, imaginative—someone who can catch an image of how this company can really soar.

How do you feel about each of these buyers? What do you like best? Least? Which one would you be most successful selling to? Whatever your feelings, you probably recognized that

- You aren't comfortable with every buyer.
- Difficulties you may have in selling some buyers may be based on differences between their expectations and yours.

TWO WAYS OF APPROACHING BUYERS

Let's consider two ways that you can approach these buyers. (See Exhibit 2.) Typically you

- Observe the buyer's body language and verbal responses to your sales approach.
- Draw conclusions about this buyer comparing them to other situations and buyers you have sold to. You tend to predict how people will behave based on past experiences.
- React to these impressions out of habit dealing with buyers and/or situations as you always have. Your impressions may or may not be correct because they're what you've been conditioned to expect.

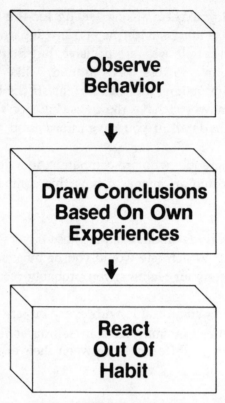

Exhibit 2   Habitual Response to Human Behavior

These rather *un*versatile reactions to your immediate impressions could cause you to

- Make rash judgments which would create misconceptions or stereotyped impressions between yourself and the buyer. You could compare him or her to unpleasant buyers whom you have met before. With this attitude, you could back away from some prospects.
- End the sales relationship without exploring the sales possibilities to their fullest because of a high level of tension.
- Create such a high tension level that problem solving would be extremely difficult, even if the relationship is continued.

Another, more versatile, approach (Exhibit 3) to buyers would be to

- Observe the buyer's behavior around two reliable measures of human behavior—assertiveness and responsiveness.

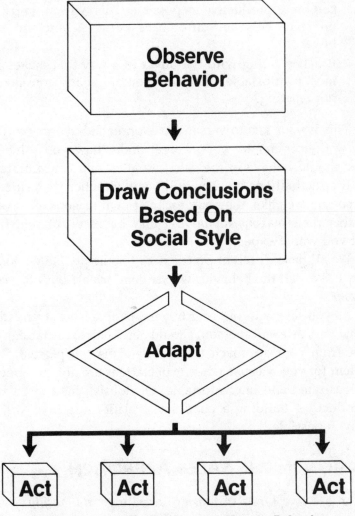

Exhibit 3   Versatile Response to Human Behavior

- Use this new awareness to draw more accurate and useful conclusions about your buyer's behavior. This means better, quicker understanding of your buyer, his preferences and expectations. You will also be more at ease with your buyer because you are acknowledging that his behavior may be different from what you have been conditioned to expect.
- Adapt your behavior to the buyer's needs so that you can be as productive as possible. This will minimize the effect of behavior differences between you and your buyer.
- Practice acting with the buyer in a way that makes him most comfortable. Note that you are acting consciously, not reacting.

This is your key to versatility: Approach buyers according to how they prefer to work. Forget about how you think the buyer should behave in the sales situation and concentrate on how they actually do act. You will begin to notice that, since no two people are alike, they buy for their own reasons, not yours, and that their reasons for buying may be very different from what you would expect.

We all have different preferences for the people we like to be with. We call the behavior we are comfortable with our *comfort zone.*

As you saw with our four buyers, people have strong ideas of how you, as a salesperson, should act. Their expectations can differ from your approach to the sale. This can present a big problem for you because when expectations are not met, people feel frustrated and uncomfortable. Obviously, this can be very unproductive. Building a good sales relationship then will be nearly impossible.

TENSION IN THE SALES APPROACH

We can see two kinds of tension in selling: *relationship tension* and *task tension. Relationship tension* is very natural. You're bringing in a new product or service—a very challenging proposition for the buyer. In addition, the buyer doesn't know anything about you. It's likely that he will be asking himself, "Are you trustworthy?" "Will your visit actually be worth his time?" "Will he be able to work with you and have faith in your follow through?"

It's up to you, the salesperson, to assure the buyer on all of these points. Making the buyer comfortable will make it easier for you to move ahead and make the sale.

Task tension is the energy required to keep the sales relationship goal directed. In other words, you can't spend too much time socializing. There is a job to be done, a goal to be achieved. Focus your energy in that direction to move along in the sales process. Watch, though, that you do not press too hard, or else you may jeopardize the relationship. Here's a look at how that might happen.

> Liz Donahue, mid-forties, is the manager of High Tech Instructional Corporation. She is in her office, angrily taking a phone call. "Is Ben Cavett here? Cavett, the sales rep from WP. How about Roger? Any progress? . . . He's still working on it? What is this, the third time this week? Four! So, how long? An hour, four hours, what? . . . He doesn't know . . . Tell the others I'm getting this thing cleared up today or we're going with another vendor . . . What? About time. Send him in."
>
> Ben Cavett, late thirties, comes in and sits down. "Hi Liz, sorry I'm late. We had a breakfast at the Madison. Quarterly awards, that sort of thing. WP sales were up 15 percent over last quarter."
>
> "Ben, the new system is giving us nothing but trouble. We've been down four times this week. Four!"
>
> "The Dominion 251?"
>
> "Yes. This down time is killing us. You've got to get that thing operational."
>
> "Uh huh. Have you had the service rep in?"
>
> "I'm tired of service reps. What we need now is serious action, not tinkering."
>
> "Uh, these new installations need time for adjustment. A sophisticated word processing system like the Dominion needs at least . . ."

"I'm not just talking about this week, Ben. Since installation we've been down almost every other day."

"Well, let's see. Installation was September 3rd, so we're talking . . ." Ben takes a look at H.T.I.C.'s installation and service record.

"Six weeks! That was six weeks ago."

". . . five-and-a-half weeks. How many service calls in that period?"

"I don't know! Too many. Ben, your follow-up on this hasn't been good at all. You don't seem to realize the problems here."

"Well, we've had a busy quarter."

"I've got two national client presentations on the 25th, and a revised generic roll-out before the 30th."

Ben studies the service record. "Ah, here's one. September 10th, and another September 12th. That's Roger Toews. Hmm."

"We are absolutely crippled without that system."

"Ah! October 2nd. October 4th. October 5th."

"I want action, now!"

"Right, well. I'll start with Roger, the service rep, get the details, see what he recommends."

"Never mind him. Talk to your manager, the president, chairman of the board—anyone, so that we can get some experts in here, fast."

"Do you remember my original recommendation that we install a dual system during the conversion period?"

"Sure. Why?"

"Well, don't you think that a dual system would have minimized this kind of problem?"

"Maybe. But it was my decision to go with the Dominion, period, so let's deal with the situation as it is."

"Well, the Dominion is very sophisticated. Has every user had instruction?"

"Ben, we're wasting time."

"Well now, you see, occasionally the users really don't understand how the system works, which means they think the system is nonoperational when it's not. It's not really the system's fault."

"Ben . . ."

"For example, if the system is slow, it could be too many terminals trying to access the same command at the same time. Then again, sometimes the printer gets hung up, and you have to initiate a recovery process. It all takes time. The Dominion has several ways of protecting itself."

"Ben, get this trouble cleared up, or we're going with another company!"

"Now wait a minute. Let's not do something here we're both going to regret. I am trying to get to the bottom of this. I would feel a lot more comfortable if we could review all the data."

"I'm not in this job to make you feel comfortable. There are at least five major companies selling what you sell, so either get that thing fixed, or WP is out the door."

"I'll get on it as soon as I can. It might take a while."

"Don't tell me about it . . . do it!"

"All right."

"Today. I want it fixed today."

"I'll give you a call as soon as I find out what's going on."

"This afternoon, Ben. Four o'clock."

Ben leaves, rather shaken. Liz, very angry, dials the phone. "Bobbi, what's the number at WP. Head office. Who's the national sales manager there. National manager. Right."

What would you do if you were Ben? Would you have done anything differently? No doubt here that Ben does little, if anything, to "develop and maintain buyer comfort throughout the sales process." No question that this is a low versatility, high tension situation. We'll follow up with the resolution of Liz's problem in a later chapter. For now, just remember that your most important responsibility is to manage both task and relationship tension so that the buyer feels comfortable and the sale moves forward productively.

THE PRODUCTIVE-TENSION ZONE

With Ben and Liz, relationship tension got so high and stressful that Liz became angrier and more frustrated than she was before the meeting. It was clear that her equipment was not going to be repaired any time soon. Ben did not do his job of satisfying the buyer's needs and task tension dropped.

What Ben didn't realize was that task tension can actually be positive, challenging. Effective problem solving could have

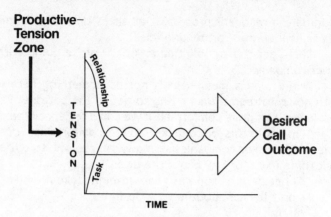

Exhibit 4   Optimal Sales Productivity

enhanced his relationship with Liz. Keeping the task and relationship tension balanced would have kept the situation on
track.

This balance is called the "Productive-Tension Zone." (See
Exhibit 4.) It is developed and maintained by the salesperson's
conscious attention to the buyer's task and relationship needs.
If you keep this in mind, you will make the most of your time
with your buyers. Your best quality sales calls happen in this
zone.

Now you have an idea of what versatility is and why it's
important in reducing tension and building your relationships
with your buyers.

Before going on to the next chapter, you may wish to assess the impact of your social style on customers. In the Appendix, pages 181 through 184 you will find three forms titled
"Impact of Social Styles on Customers." Using these forms,
think about the positive and negative effect your style may
have on customers, and how it may be helping or hindering
your overall sales effectiveness.

In Chapter 2, we will start to define different social styles
and show how knowing about them can help you to be more
productive in your sales approach.

2

Behavior: The Key to Social Styles

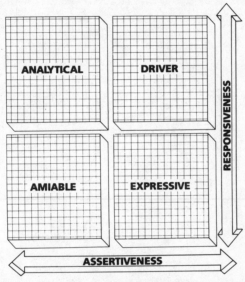

"Learning about social styles changed things greatly for me. When I started out as an account executive, it was very helpful to me to understand how people perceived me. I didn't realize that some of my customers saw me as too talkative and not businesslike enough. My knowledge of social styles gave me important information on how I came across to my clients," says an account manager.

H̲ow you, the salesperson, and the buyer come across—how you behave in the sales situation—is certainly important. Understanding this process is vital for you to sell more effectively.

When you meet a buyer, you immediately notice behavior. That is, you see the person's gestures and expressions. You hear the person's voice and use of words. Very quickly you sense whether or not you like this person.

Even though we know that people are made up of thoughts, feelings, and behaviors, it is highly unlikely that whatever he thinks and feels privately about all this will be shared with you. At this moment, then, your main concern is only what you can see and hear. It is his behavior that you respond to, and that behavior is a direct indication about the person's social style. (See Exhibit 1.)

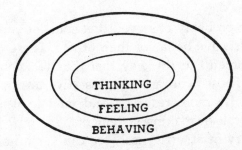

Exhibit 1   Behavior Is an Indication of Social Style

WHAT IS BEHAVIOR?

When you meet other people, you notice how they talk. That is, is their voice monotone or inflected? Do they walk ramrod straight or do they walk casually? Are their movements fast or slow? Do they seem to carry computerbanks of facts in their heads or do you wonder, from their dramatic actions, if they were ever on Broadway? All these things tell us something of what to expect from them.

Researchers have come up with a variety of concepts about what behavior really is. Unfortunately, they haven't always arrived at the same conclusions. They have been able to agree, however, that two dimensions of human behavior can be observed and measured. These dimensions are *assertiveness* and *responsiveness*. Let us take a look at what this means.

Assertiveness

Assertiveness is the degree to which a person is perceived as attempting to influence the thoughts and actions of others.

We should mention that assertiveness isn't a trait or quality. So you should not look at it as something that is either good or bad. It is just a way for you to describe how you perceive your customers' behavior, or, for that matter, how they perceive yours.

You have probably observed that some of your prospects show more assertive behavior than others. These people tend to be more forceful in the way that they tell you what they have to say. Those who are less assertive are not as direct. They are usually more reserved and tend to listen and ask questions instead of making statements. To show how different people vary in assertiveness, we can use a horizontal assertiveness scale. (See Exhibit 2.) It is an easy-to-use tool for measuring how a person is perceived as attempting to influence others.

We can diagram this by placing their behavior on a continuum that illustrates degrees of assertiveness. Keep in mind as we do this that we are not judging any behavior as good or bad, right or wrong. We are not trying to figure out the inner person either—his or her motivations, hopes, and so forth. What we are doing is simply observing the buyer's behavior. (See Exhibit 2.)

On one side of the scale we are placing those people who are perceived as being *Ask-Assertive*. These are people who ask more than tell. When this person does make a statement, his tone of voice might sound more like an open-ended question than a directly stated idea. Take, for instance, Buyer 1 on page 8 who said, "I always feel it's awkward when people have

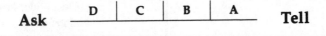

Perceptions of Ask-Assertive Behavior:	Perceptions of Tell-Assertive Behavior:
Seldom uses voice to emphasize ideas	Empasizes ideas by tone change
Expressions and posture are quiet and submissive	Expressions are aggressive or dominant
Deliberate, studied, or slow in speech	Quick, clear, or fast paced
Indifferent handshake	Firm handshakes
Asks questions more often than makes statements	Makes statements more often than asks questions
Vague, unclear about what is wanted	Lets one know what is wanted
Tends to lean backwards	Tends to lean forward to make a point

Exhibit 2   Guidelines for Recognition of Social Styles Based on Perceptions of Assertiveness

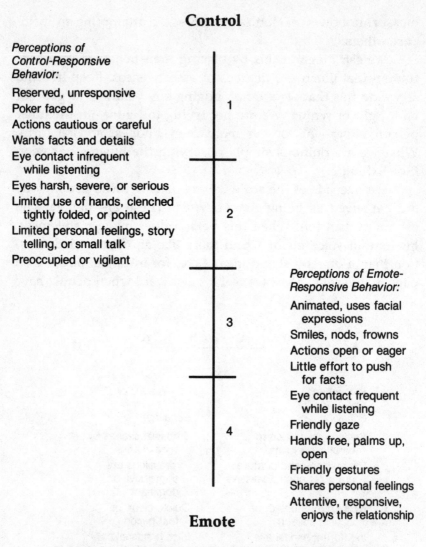

Control

Perceptions of Control-Responsive Behavior:

Reserved, unresponsive
Poker faced
Actions cautious or careful
Wants facts and details
Eye contact infrequent
   while listening
Eyes harsh, severe, or serious
Limited use of hands, clenched
   tightly folded, or pointed
Limited personal feelings, story
   telling, or small talk
Preoccupied or vigilant

1

2

3

4

Perceptions of Emote-Responsive Behavior:

Animated, uses facial
   expressions
Smiles, nods, frowns
Actions open or eager
Little effort to push
   for facts
Eye contact frequent
   while listening
Friendly gaze
Hands free, palms up,
   open
Friendly gestures
Shares personal feelings
Attentive, responsive,
   enjoys the relationship

Emote

**Exhibit 3 Guidelines for Recognition of Social Styles
Based on Perceptions of Responsiveness**

hidden agendas, don't you?" and "You know, isn't sales essentially communications?"

Ask-Assertive people sometimes speak more deliberately, or even cautiously. Remember Jeff Holte? "Would it be all right if I started by telling you a little about Clark-Data? . . . Clark was founded fifteen years ago by four people who all came out of the banking industry."

You may notice the Ask-Assertive person lean back in his chair and he may not have direct eye contact with you when he talks. Jeff Holte does this by looking more at his display than the buyer. All of his charts and figures help him to minimize the risk of misstating facts in his relatively slow, methodical presentation. Any change in his sales script does not come from any spontaneous idea from him, but instead from questions or statements from the buyer.

On the other hand, a *Tell-Assertive* person will take more of an active role in the sales situation. He'll probably lean forward and maintain direct eye contact. Although the Tell-Assertive person states rather than asks, if he does ask a question, the tone is apt to be abrupt. He might be rather competitive with you in an attempt to take charge of the call. In Jeff Holte's meeting with Hal, we saw Hal actually interrupt Jeff's presentation.

Jeff: Now, let's compare a conventional on-line ATM against Clark's.

Hal: Say, you know something, I think Bob Sharkey should hear this. C'mon, let's go down to his office.

Jeff: Well, uh, sure . . . uh . . .

Remember that although Jeff Holte lost control of this presentation because of his Ask-Assertiveness, the same level of assertiveness gained a sale for him from Garth. There is no correct degree of assertiveness. What is important is that you find the right level for each situation.

Responsiveness

The other way to measure behavior is by observing responsiveness.

Responsiveness is the degree to which a person is perceived as expressing feelings when relating to others.

As with assertiveness, we have a scale to measure the degree of a person's responsiveness. (See Exhibit 3.)

With responsiveness, we are looking at how people express themselves and how they react. There are two ways of describing this aspect of a person's behavior. There are those people who control their emotions and those who are more emotive.

We met Ben Cavett, a salesperson, in Chapter 1. Although his customer became quite angry and upset, Ben tends to control his own emotions—almost to the point of being aloof about the situation. He doesn't respond well to Liz's demand to get the system fixed. Instead, Ben focuses on details and facts to resolve the problem.

Ben, as a Control-Responsive person, does not show his own feelings. He wants to get the job done, but his deliberate, systematic approach is not necessarily as speedy as Liz would like.

The Control-Responsive buyer is the one who would say to a salesperson, "I would prefer to deal with you in a businesslike manner. That's not to say I wouldn't like to visit, but time is important."

The Emote-Responsive person, like Hal in Jeff's second sales situation, does show his or her feelings. This buyer likes dealing with people. He'd say, "I'm more receptive when salespeople are relaxed and able to show concern for me and my problems," or "With him you get a strong feeling for the person you're dealing with. He understands me and my department." This person will use intuition and imagination as much as the cold facts in making a buying decision.

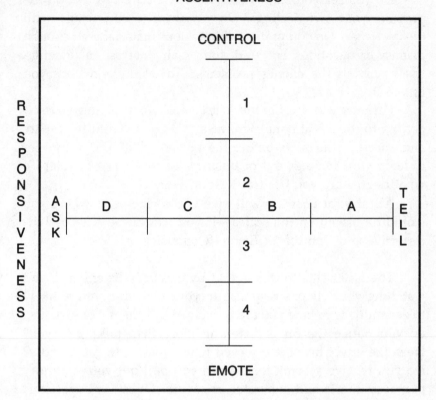

ASSERTIVENESS

Exhibit 4   The Making of the Social Style Matrix

In looking at Exhibit 4 you might find it interesting to place yourself on the assertiveness and responsiveness scales. You might do this by self-observation, that is, by watching your own behavior in the sales situation. One note of caution: There is a good chance that you won't see yourself as others do. Keep this in mind as you assess your own behavior.

Are you *Tell-Assertive?* Do you hear yourself authoritatively telling your client in a loud voice about your product or service? Is your speech fast? To what degree are you Tell-Assertive?

Are you *Ask-Assertive?* Do you ask your buyer about his needs? Is your speech soft and relatively slow? To what degree are you Ask-Assertive?

Do you see yourself as *Emote-Responsive?* Do you enjoy expressing your own feelings? Do you want to be friendly with the customer? Do you prefer to know your material well enough to answer questions but find your main interest in imaginatively solving the client's problems? To what degree are you Emote-Responsive?

Perhaps you are *Control-Responsive?* Do you find yourself getting to the job at hand right away? Do you carefully prepare and analyze your facts before the presentation? Do you prefer to keep your feelings out of business as much as possible? To what degree are you Control-Responsive?

All of your answers will give you a clue as to where you would be placed on the scales—if you tend to be Ask- or Tell-Assertive and Control- or Emote-Responsive.

The other side to this is that by carefully listening to and watching your client's response to your behavior, you're likely to get a hint as to how you are perceived by others. For instance, do you notice the buyer listening more than talking to you? Does the buyer become reserved when you try to get friendly? Do you receive a blank look when you pull out your carefully prepared charts and computer printouts? Does the buyer start talking about family when you want to close the sale? Your observations along these lines are good indicators of how you are seen by your customers.

Even though we are not judging degrees of assertive and responsive behavior, we all know that there are some people who we just feel uneasy with. You can probably guess that, compared with you, these people are usually on the opposite end of the assertiveness and/or responsiveness scale. For instance, an Emote-Responsive salesperson may have difficulty relating to a Control-Responsive client—they are not equally comfortable with showing emotion. As a salesperson, you know that it's vital that you get along with your customers. This is why it's especially important for you to learn how to be versatile in your work.

This is where your responsibility for maintaining productive tension in the situation comes in. With task and relationship tension in balance, there is a good chance that you will succeed in keeping a productive sales relationship with your customer. When, however, tension is allowed to get out of hand because of differences in assertiveness and responsiveness, you might lose the client. At best, you and your client will make a truce for the necessity of his buying your product or service—until he is able to find another supplier. Now, let's take another look at Liz Donahue (a Tell-Assertive, Control-Response buyer) and Ben Cavett (an Ask-Assertive, Control-Response salesperson) to see how they are able to become more versatile problem solvers. When we saw them in Chapter 1, Ben had difficulty in understanding Liz's situation with the breakdown of the new word processing system. As things turned out, Liz remained angry, Ben's sales manager was about to receive a negative report, the system was still down, and there was a good chance that WP would be replaced by another vendor. When we see them now, Ben, though not perfect, has a much better time maintaining a productive comfort zone.

> Ben enters Liz's office at H.T.I.C. As a senior executive responsible for results, Liz is very upset and anxious about the problems she's having with the word processing system that she bought from Ben.
>
> "Ben, the new system is giving us nothing but trouble. We've been down four times this week. Four."
>
> "The Dominion 251?"
>
> "Yes. This down time is killing us. You've got to get that thing operational."
>
> "Uh huh. Have you had the service rep in?"
>
> "I'm tired of service reps. What we need now is serious action, not tinkering."
>
> "Well, these new installations need time for adjustment. A sophisticated word processing system like the Dominion needs at least . . ."
>
> "I'm not just talking about this week, Ben. Since installation we've been down almost every other day."
>
> "Well, let's see. Installation was September 3rd, so we're talking . . ."
>
> "Six weeks! That was six weeks ago."

Now we see Ben become more responsive to Liz's problem, more versatile than he was in the first example.

> "It's hard to believe it's been that long. Liz, I'm really sorry. I had no idea . . ."
>
> Liz, too, expresses her feelings more directly. "Your follow-up on this hasn't been too good, Ben. You don't seem to realize the problems here."
>
> "Well, we've had a very busy quarter, but that's no excuse, I realize that."
>
> "We're absolutely crippled without that system. I've got two national client presentations on the 25th, and a revised generic roll-out before the 30th. I want action, now."
>
> Ben begins to understand what he has to do. "Right. I'll start with Roger, the service rep, get the details, see what he recommends. Then, there's a designer at corporate headquarters who set up the 251. I'll get him out here to troubleshoot the installation."
>
> "I thought I bought a system without bugs."
>
> "Liz, every new installation has a few problems. Now, are you sure we're not just talking about a training issue here?"
>
> "Everyone was trained."
>
> "Well, the Dominion is very sophisticated."
>
> "Ben, we're wasting time."
>
> Ben realizes that he's lapsing into his Ask-Assertive behavior. "OK. Can you set me up with a phone and a desk?"
>
> "Sure."
>
> Ben is gaining control of the situation by being versatile. His actions become more Tell-Assertive. "Now, first, I'll cancel the rest of my appointments, then I'll get the office to take Roger off his planned maintenance calls."
>
> Ben's versatility is evident in Liz's change to more Ask-Assertive behavior. "What for?"
>
> "Well, we'll keep him here. If anything goes down, he'll fix it. In the meantime, I'll call Corporate and get Mike Plant out here by tomorrow noon."
>
> "Mike Plant?"
>
> "The designer. The expert."
>
> "Oh, right."
>
> "Now Liz, I know you're very upset, but I will get to the bottom of this. Now, where can I make these calls?"
>
> Liz arranges for Ben to use a desk. "OK. You've got a phone. How much time will you need?"

"Well, I'll get back to you as soon as I find out what's going on."

"Tomorrow, Ben. Four o'clock."

"Four o'clock, Liz."

Notice here how Ben's versatility not only earned him a day more than in the previous example to solve the problem, but it also strengthened his relationship with Liz. Liz is not exactly happy, but she is at least cooperative. Both people can live with the results of this meeting.

ASSERTIVENESS AND RESPONSIVENESS: KEYS TO SOCIAL STYLE

Now that you've seen the assertiveness and responsiveness scales, all we have to do is put them together and identify the person's social style. This will give you an idea of what that buyer is really like and how you can meet his or her expectations.

We create what we call a *Social Style Matrix* by placing the vertical responsiveness scale over the horizontal assertiveness scale. This forms quadrants. You can define your own and your clients' behavior by where it falls in the matrix. (See Exhibit 5.)

The matrix represents a tool for organizing descriptions of the four basic social styles: *Analytical, Driver, Expressive* and *Amiable.* By referring to the matrix, you can anticipate how your buyers will prefer to do business. To show how this works, we see that the

- Analytical is Ask-Assertive and Control-Responsive.
- Driver is Tell-Assertive and Control-Responsive.
- Expressive is Tell-Assertive and Emote-Responsive.
- Amiable is Ask-Assertive and Emote-Responsive.

People in each of the four social styles may want the same results, but each social style has a different way of behaving when it comes to buying and selling. Looking at the differences

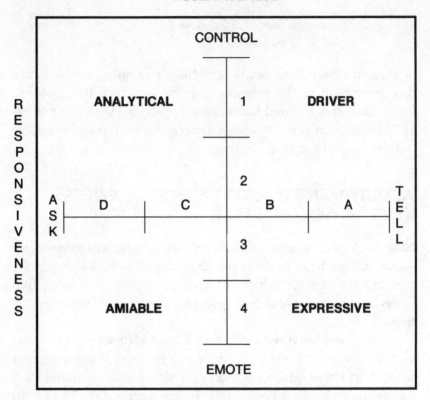

Exhibit 5   The Social Styles Matrix

in social styles this way, it certainly is obvious why there is so much potential for problems in sales relationships. Reasons for the problems may not be altogether obvious. We could say that, given two people with different social styles, one may have been told that it is healthy to show emotion while the other, as a child, may have been taught to keep a stiff upper lip. One may have received awards for achievement, while the other may have been ridiculed for trying to get ahead. The way that these people responded to their environment has, by the time you meet them, become a habit, a comfortable way to respond to any similar situation.

Whatever the reasons for their behavior may be, in the sales situation, what we see is what we have to assume they are. If a buyer indicates a need for more facts, we give her more facts. If a buyer wants to discuss how the new computer network will affect the morale of his staff, we give him facts about another company where the morale was actually raised because of the improvement in staff communication.

All this means that you are a versatile salesperson—that you recognize the four social styles and that you are able to respond to the needs of each one. This does not mean that you try to change your style or that you put on your Expressive mask when you meet an Expressive. This could be very tiresome for you and for your client. If you are acting and your act is detected, your credibility will be in doubt.

It is your job to be aware of productive tension and how to maintain it while keeping the buyer's task and relationship needs in focus. By doing this, you are not becoming another person. You're just temporarily modifying your style to adapt your assertiveness and responsiveness to fit the needs of the situation. This is versatility.

Before you can do any of this, you have to learn to recognize a person's social style. For practice, try to figure out in which quadrant you'd probably find these well-known people. Be sure you look separately at their assertiveness and responsiveness before naming a style for them. This prevents confusion and "pigeon holing."

1. John McEnroe
2. Jimmy Carter
3. Barbara Walters
4. Ronald Reagan

5. Queen Elizabeth II
6. Dwight Eisenhower
7. Tom Landry
8. Billie Jean King

Note: For assessments, see end of chapter, p. 39.

How did you do? To get a better notion of why, say, Reagan is perceived as an Expressive and Walters, a Driver, let's take a look at each of the four social types.

Analyticals

**I like someone who is thorough and precise,
basically well-prepared and organized. I like
getting it down on paper.**

Starting with the quadrant in the upper left of the matrix, we have a person who is perceived as being Control-Responsive and Ask-Assertive. For the Analytical details and facts are often persuasive. Analyticals are more comfortable with concepts and complex situations.

Analyticals like to know where they are going, and may proceed carefully when taking that next step. Because they are cautious, they tend to make their buying decisions on facts and evidence.

They are seen as placing their priority on the task to be accomplished rather than on the relationship. In other words, their Analytical social style tends to combine Ask-Assertiveness with emotional reserve in dealing with other people.

Drivers

**Show me that you understand my problem, and
then tell me what your product or service can do.
But don't box me in. Give me options, choices.**

Now, in the upper right quadrant, we have a person who is perceived as being Control-Responsive and Tell-Assertive—a Driver. Drivers are most comfortable when they are able to control themselves and their work environment. Drivers want quick action and tangible results.

The Driver's priority is to see that the job gets done and, as a result, is perceived as working at a quick pace. Drivers usually behave as though they know exactly what they want and where they are going. Generally speaking, the Driver's social style tends to combine Tell-Assertive directness with emotional control when dealing with other people.

Expressive

I like salespeople who are decisive, but that doesn't mean we can't take the time to toss ideas around. I like that, so don't pressure me into making a decision right off the bat.

In the lower right quadrant is the Expressive. This social style is characterized by behavior that is Tell-Assertive and Emote-Responsive. Expressives are not at all hesitant about making their presence and their feelings known. They are generally very enthusiastic.

Like the Driver, Expressives move at a fast pace, but unlike the Driver, Expressives place a priority on getting results through interpersonal relationships. Expressives can be highly persuasive when they combine personal power with emotional display.

Expressives are perceived as highly intuitive and may give the impression that they are not interested in hard data. Research indicates, however, that Expressives do use data if only to validate their instincts.

Amiables

I want to know I'm working with an effective problem solver who has solid product knowledge. And most of all, give me assurance that what you're proposing will benefit me and my people.

The quadrant in the lower left describes people who are Ask-Assertive and Emote-Responsive. This is the Amiable social style. Amiables tend to share their emotions openly. Their behavior also may suggest little desire to impose their actions and perhaps their ideas on others.

Amiables project sensitivity to other people's feelings, and therefore take time to establish personal relationships. They are supportive of others, and use relationships to achieve results.

Amiables appear to relate openly with people, and invest the energy to ask questions which, they hope, will get to the core of the matter. At times, Amiables may appear deliberate, even cautious. The Amiable social style combines Ask-Assertive reserve with emotional expression when dealing with others.

THE QUADRANT WITHIN

If we consider everyone's social style, we discover that each quadrant has an equal number of people—25 percent of the population for each social style. Knowing this, you may be wondering, "Well, if there are only four types, why is it that in real life there are so many kinds of people? Take Michael, for instance. He always must have facts and figures before he'll buy, but every time I call on him he's willing to spend time on small talk. I suspect he's an Analytical, but . . ."

You are right. Michael is probably an Analytical who shows Amiable behavior, an Amiable-Analytical. There are variations within each social style. We show this by further subdividing the quadrants into 16 social style quadrants (Exhibit 6). This means that each quadrant has its own responsiveness and assertiveness scales. Just as with the larger matrix, each smaller one has a quadrant for each social style.

By using the 16 subquadrants, we can describe a person's dominant characteristics as well as pinpoint his or her variations in behavior. This is how it works.

> Jeanne is a friendly, cooperative buyer who listens politely to your sales presentation. As she starts to feel more at ease

D	C	B	A	
D-1 Analytical Analytical	C-1 Driving Analytical	B-1 Analytical Driver	A-1 Driving Driver	**1**
D-2 Amiable Analytical	C-2 Expressive Analytical	B-2 Amiable Driver	A-2 Expressive Driver	**2**
D-3 Analytical Amiable	C-3 Driving Amiable	B-3 Analytical Expressive	A-3 Driving Expressive	**3**
D-4 Amiable Amiable	C-4 Expressive Amiable	B-4 Amiable Expressive	A-4 Expressive Expressive	**4**

Exhibit 6   The Sixteen Subquadrants

with you, she asks questions, usually having to do with how your system has been accepted at other companies. You assure her that acceptance has been very positive and that you guarantee personal follow-through with every installation. She needs time to talk over your system with her staff, but you detect that she is definitely interested in buying. Why? Because she is becoming much more animated and confident in telling you how your system is just what she's been looking for.

You suspect that Jeanne is an Expressive-Amiable. Her dominant behavior is within the Amiable quadrant. She is, however, slightly more Tell-Assertive than Ask-Assertive and much more Emote-Responsive than Control-Responsive.

Jim tells you upfront that he has called a meeting with his department heads for 2:30—that's in half an hour. You adjust your presentation to his time limits. Whenever you think you've made a point, he challenges you with a question. After twenty-five minutes, you're barely through half of your presentation when you notice that he's tapping his fingers on his desk. Then he asks you for more details—where your numbers are and exactly what can he expect from your company. You thought you had covered this, or would have if he had given you the chance. Before he leaves for his meeting, you agree to send him a printout that clearly shows what results he will get with the system.

Jim shows the dominant behavior of a Driver. He seems to be, however, more Ask-Assertive and Control-Responsive than most Drivers so we would call him an Analytical Driver.

Another example is Winnie, a boutique owner who enjoys telling you about her special fashion expertise.

Winnie talks fast, especially when she's excited about her store, which is usually the case. Her customers like the boutique's clothes as much as Winnie's conversation. Sometimes her spontaneity detracts from your attempt to show her your new line. As you write up her order, she seems to be imagining just how this particular outfit will look on that particular customer.

As you pack up to leave, you casually mention that you noticed that there's a new shopping mall in another town that has a store for rent. Rather abruptly she tells you that she's been planning to open a new store. It's part of her five-year plan. You must stay and tell her the facts. Winnie is an Expressive-Expressive.

You can practice using the subquadrants by looking for a person's dominant behavior. This will tell you which of the four social styles this person might be. Then look for subtle differences in assertiveness and responsiveness when he or she is compared to others you have known of the same style. These differences give you a more specific subquadrant profile of that person's social style.

This chapter should get you started with understanding why social style gives you a good tool for dealing with your customers. If you know a person's social style, you'll have a much better chance of predicting how he or she will respond in the sales situation. You will be better prepared to adapt your selling behavior and influence the direction of the meeting. Your clients will be more comfortable with you and you will have a chance to build a good, lasting relationship.

Let's practice, then, what you have learned about social style identification. Go to the form in the Appendix entitled "Social Styles Identification," and use it to come up with the social style of at least ten of your prospects. This will help you apply your readings about social styles in the following chapters.

Next, we'll start taking a more in-depth view of each social style. You'll get to see exactly what each one wants from a salesperson and how you can use versatility to build good sales relationships.

Assessments (see p. 33)

1. Expressive; 2. Amiable; 3. Driver; 4. Expressive; 5. Analytical; 6. Amiable; 7. Analytical; 8. Driver.

3

The Analytical: "Practical Suggestions Are What I Need"

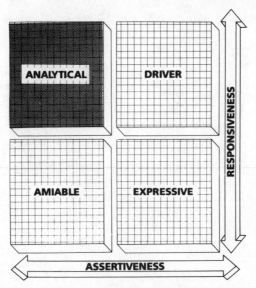

"When I go out on a sales call, I want to make sure that I take all the backup information that I think I'll need. I also research specific points that might be of value to the individual customer. Even if the customer doesn't ask about all this, I'm glad to know that I have it so that I can answer most, if not all, questions that can come up. I feel good about doing my job this way." This is the typical view of an Analytical salesperson on making sales presentations.

The Analytical social style is shown in the Ask-Assertive and Control-Responsive quadrant in the matrix. (See Exhibit 1.) It could be that your Analytical customer seems, to you, to be your most reserved buyer. The fact that his facial expressions tend to be unchanging and that he doesn't gesture very much may make his body language difficult to "read." His verbal responses may tend to be subdued, too. You may, at times, wonder if this buyer is responding to your presentation at all. You may find yourself trying to draw responses from him.

You may think that it is altogether natural for you to show reasonable enthusiasm for your product or service. The Analytical, however, may be a bit put off by all this. He may see your excitement as distracting and unprofessional. At least in the beginning of the sales process, he would prefer that you present

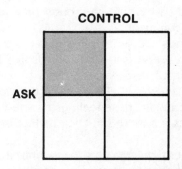

Exhibit 1   The Analytical Buyer

yourself as more businesslike in your sales relationship with him. You can certainly be cordial with him, just not overly friendly. For this buyer your down-to-earth businesslike presentation is important.

> Sherry, an Analytical in charge of data processing at a bank, called Ron's company when she saw its literature on hardware accessories for computers, such as printer stands, disk file boxes, and so forth. She thought that the addition of some of these new accesories might raise the morale and productivity of her staff.
>
> Ron, an Expressive salesperson, is very excited about his line. Although he is relatively new at selling these products, he has seen his printer stands do everything from cutting down on eye strain to saving office space. He believes in the usefulness of his product.
>
> He meets Sherry in her office, which is functionally furnished in standard modern style with little decoration. Actually, most of the decoration he sees are data printouts and schedule sheets. Sherry is very polite and businesslike. She has his company's brochures on her desk.
>
> Just before meeting with Sherry, Ron had sold many of the products in his line to an accounting firm across town. He is very "up" about the sale. Soon after introducing himself to Sherry, he tells her about how happy the accounting firm was with its purchase. To this, she listens politely but doesn't respond. She does not know this firm and does not see how this is of any relevance to her situation.
>
> She asks Ron about his latest series of printer stands. She is adding more staff members and computer hardware to her department and this would be a good time to update some of her accessory equipment.
>
> These stands are what he is especially proud of selling. He makes his presentation with words like "best," "easiest," "most convenient," and "most efficient" freely mixed in his discussion. He sincerely believes all of this about his products and wants to convey these feelings to Sherry. He thinks that if she can get as interested in the product as he is, she surely will buy.
>
> Sherry listens quietly until he is finished. Then, she asks him to explain what he meant by all those superlatives. She

would like to know the facts behind the words. More specifically, she'd like to know what this means for her situation.

Ron thought he had explained all this. He begins to get a little impatient and then enthusiastically tells her that she can call five other customers for reference. All of them are as excited about the products as he is and will gladly discuss them with her.

Sherry is silent for a moment. She goes back to asking him for facts, like what are the sizes of the several models. Ron tells her not to worry, there is a size for every office. She should have no problem.

Ron lets her know that if she orders today she can get a reasonable introductory discount. He senses that she needs the printer stands and may as well make a purchase commitment now. Sherry asks him to leave her more information. She is not ready to make a decision.

Friendly enthusiasm doesn't usually work, at first anyway, because the Analytical customer is task oriented. Although he may open up and become friendlier with you later on as the sales relationship develops, his main concern now is to get the job done. And to him, getting the job done means that he will want to take the time to analyze all the information that you can possibly offer him.

This buyer is certainly Ask-Assertive when it comes to requesting details about your product or service. Be prepared for this when you make your call on him. Anticipate all the questions you can that may arise from your presentation. Then come ready with all the background information, specifications, brochures, and printouts that you can think of. You might even consider bringing along an expert or two.

Lee, an Amiable salesperson, is an expert in his area of industrial chemicals. He sells chemicals to agricultural product manufacturers. His company has developed a chemical that can be used in the manufacture of a new, safe pesticide.

He has been presenting this innovative chemical to several companies with mixed results. Today, it is Walt's turn to hear about it. Walt is an Analytical buyer. He works closely with the product development people at his manufacturing company. Walt and the development staff members all have highly technical backgrounds.

Walt has already read information about this new chemical. He's moderately interested. This is not so much because of the innovative aspects of the product but because it is less expensive than other products and that might help his company's sagging bottom line.

During his presentation, Lee highlights some of the environmental bonuses of his product. He likes Walt's attentiveness and patience. He realizes that this sales process will take some time to develop, but he feels that he's getting a good start.

Walt is still interested but Lee hasn't really covered those points that are of most value to his situation. He asks Lee about specific costs. Lee gives him some printouts with related information.

They both take a look at the numbers. Walt thinks that they have to be more specific for his situation. He gives Lee some more information to use for coming up with new numbers that will specifically help him. He tells Lee that he cannot proceed without seeing the new data and discussing the specs of the new chemical with the product development staff.

Lee gets the information to Walt in two days. At that time, he sets up another meeting with Walt. When they meet, Walt has run Lee's data through his computer and has come up with some more questions. Lee is frankly baffled by some of them. Instead of taking the chance of answering incorrectly, Lee offers to schedule another meeting to which he'll bring one of the technical experts from his company.

Walt brings one of his product developers to this next meeting. Both he and Walt are very interested in the new chemical for different reasons. Walt likes the data on the new printouts that Lee has brought. The product developer likes the innovative quality of the new chemical and what that might mean in the marketplace. A few days after this last meeting, Walt calls Lee with a decision to purchase.

Even though you may provide much information, there's a good chance that the Analytical buyer will think of something else to ask of you. Whether or not you personally have a thorough knowledge of your product information, always get answers to the Analytical's questions. There may be times that you will have to call on experts to respond to the Analytical's need for facts. Remember that he is depending on your giving him this information so that he can make a purchase decision. Your cooperation with him will strengthen the sales relationship.

Actually, the Analytical buyer will expect a little something more than random facts and figures. Your organization of these details is very important. How well-organized you are can have an effect on how you influence the buyer. Your logically ordered plan can create a positive impression. It will show that you have taken the time to adapt the facts to the specifics of this buyer's needs.

If you are, say, an Expressive or an Amiable and find yourself tuning out, catch yourself. You may feel that this customer is asking too many technical questions. He would like for you to listen to him and follow his reasoning. Show that you are interested in these details, too, because they are, in fact, part of your package.

In this case, your social style will help him to see the big picture. He may become so bogged down in looking at the leaves that he misses the forest. Give him a descriptive view of how all the details of your offer work together. Keep in mind that he will always be more interested in the individual facts. He will believe that they actually allow him to understand the "whole" picture—to him, a more comprehensive view than yours. However, your approach will help him see your offer from a different perspective.

Anne, an Analytical office manager at an insurance company, wants to buy electronic typewriters for her staff. Up to now, they have used standard electric typewriters. Although she is rather conservative in her approach to business, she feels that it's time to look into something technologically advanced, but she is not ready for a word processing system.

Rita, a Driver salesperson, carries lines of typewriters and word processing systems. She prefers to sell word processors and cannot understand why, given Anne's office setup, she would not want a word processing system. At any rate, she'd like to make a sale—no matter what the product is.

Rita presents both lines—the word processors and electronic typewriters—during her first meeting with Anne. At the point that she thinks Anne would be interested in how word processors would be her better choice, Rita notices that Anne is not really listening. Actually, the only response that she can see is that Anne has shifted away from her slightly and has crossed her arms in front of her as if she's resisting the discussion.

Rita asks Anne if she has any questions so far. Anne responds that she'd like to know more about the electronic typewriters, their cost, specifications and availability—in other words, everything that she wanted to know at the beginning of the presentation.

In an attempt to tone down her enthusiasm for what she would decide were she in Anne's position, Rita listens more closely to Anne's needs. Yes, she does want electronic typewriters, however, she should be aware that sometime in the future she might want to go to word processors. Rita shows Anne how a particular model of electronic typewriter that is well-suited to Anne's needs would make a good printer for word processors if, down the line, she should want to invest in those.

She leaves product and cost information with Anne. The following week she gets a call—Anne is ready to buy. Anne likes the idea of not only getting what she wants now but also getting an option for a future system.

In some circumstances, the Analytical buyer's rather intense consideration of the facts can cause a delay in the sales process. Be aware that this can happen. The Analytical may have a problem coming up with a final buying decision. There may always be more facts that he'll want to look at, more options he'll want to analyze. Give him the facts that he wants but constantly relate them to the issue of his larger needs. It will be up to you to keep the process moving.

Louis is an Amiable salesperson for a line of personal hygiene products—soap, toothpaste, shampoo, etc.—that has, until now, been sold only through healthfood stores. The products have done quite well through those retail channels. It reinvested its profits to build up its research, development, manufacturing, and marketing. It has grown from being a typical "garage" enterprise to having its own offices and plant.

The company has done a good job of saturating the healthfood market with its products. In order to grow, it has to reach other markets. The marketing people have determined that now is the time to go into drugstores. They would especially like for the products to be taken by chain stores.

This is why Louis is trying to schedule a meeting with Sheila. She is an Analytical buyer for a large regional chain of drugstores. He has phoned her; however, she has refused to see him because his company has what she considers to be a "healthfood stigma." She does not understand how these products could fit into a "normal" drugstore. She perceives them as being too radically different.

Louis decides to send her a detailed letter explaining his company's new approach to marketing and developing its products. He includes a wealth of product information materials. When he does a followup phone call, Sheila is more receptive. She has read the information and will schedule a meeting.

After his presentation, Sheila has many questions dealing with the quality of the products. She wants to make sure that the products meet industry standards, that they are not, in fact, made in kitchen tubs.

Louis is unable to give Sheila all the specifics that she needs to make a purchasing decision. Although she has been polite, Louis is also feeling the sting of some of her comments about the way she has perceived his company's product lines. So, he decides to bring in his research and manufacturing experts to the next meeting.

At that time, he allows the experts to do most of the talking. This is apparently what Sheila needs to hear. They seem to adequately answer her questions. Finally, he leaves more detailed product information for her to read.

She does not get back to him. He schedules another meeting to show her the new packaging that his marketing people have come up with in line with their new approach to selling. This interests her. She asks about costs and discounts so that she can discuss these with her staff.

Soon after her staff meeting, she lets him know that she is interested in discussing the purchase agreement. This sales process had taken months to complete, however Louis's patience was worthwhile.

One way to keep the sales process moving is for you to research not only the buyer's individual needs, but also to consider what the overall needs of his company may be. That can include any business activity that might have an influence on the Analytical's decision. Since the Analytical tends to be conservative in his decisionmaking, he will not want to disrupt his company's policy.

> Caroline, the Analytical owner-manager of one store in a quick print franchise chain, needs to update her copier equipment. She asks three print equipment companies to send sales representatives. She is particularly interested in the equipment made by Roy's company because she has seen the specs on a copier that looks just right for her business.
>
> When he calls on her in her small back office, she clearly understands what the copier is and what it can do. Mainly, what she is interested in knowing is how much it will cost. Roy quotes her full price and Caroline suddenly clams up. She tells him that she'll have to take time to think about it and will get back to him.
>
> Outside, Roy notices that there is a large poster in her window stating that all the print shops in the franchise chain charge five cents a copy. He realizes that his quote was too high for Caroline to keep her costs in line.
>
> Roy gets his financial experts to come up with a payment plan that will allow Caroline to maintain a reasonable profit on the copies produced by his company's equipment. He also works out a package that will, in effect, give her a discount.
>
> He sends her this new information, and is surprised when she calls him the day she receives it. The new numbers look fine to her and she'd like to discuss the purchase agreement.

Consider company guidelines. Ask yourself, for instance, are there any established policies that are followed by the buyer's company that can have an effect on the way he sees your proposal? Are there any purchasing guidelines that he must work within? Does the company have any goals that have to coincide with the buyer's own objectives? Does your offer, in any way, threaten what he perceives to be good about the status quo at his company?

Your ability to answer these questions will help you to work constructively with this buyer. The Analytical tends to be conservative in his decision making. He will try not to make waves within the system. This does not mean that he won't accept a creative solution to his problem. It is just that he prefers that the solution be based on solid facts and that it works closely within the bounds of what is generally accepted in his organization.

If you show respect for the Analytical's attention to detail and his well-disciplined approach to getting the job done, you should not have much of a problem in developing a positive sales relationship with him. He will trust you if you are accurate and use common sense in your presentation of your product or service.

He will respect you if you are able to support his ideas, which he sees as logical common sense. If things are going well, you may even notice that, although he will still tend to be reserved, this customer is becoming friendlier. If things are not going well, he'll become more reserved.

You will know if the Analytical is uncomfortable in the sales situation. He will try to withdraw from it or change the subject. You will have to be able to notice this yourself because he will probably not directly state what is bothering him as would the Driver or the Expressive. He may simply tell you that he needs more time to think about your offer or that he is very busy and has to get back to work. Either way you might be losing the sale. He'll want no further discussion. Here's an example.

> Paul Michaels is an Analytical executive in his early thirties. His office is comfortably furnished, complete with artwork and a computer terminal. Both he and Terry Joseph, a salesperson in his late twenties, are wearing conservative gray business suits.

Terry, an Expressive, is discussing a proposal on a company benefits package that he has made to Paul. Both are holding copies of it. Paul would like to have some aspects of the proposal explained in detail.

". . . so a major concern for us is what kind of turnaround time a company normally experiences at the time an insured suffers a loss." Paul would like to know the specific turnaround time.

"We normally don't have trouble with turnaround. We're a very responsive company." The Expressive Terry is not especially interested in mentioning the exact time period. It's enough for him to know that the plan works.

"Also, your pricing structure isn't as competitive as I might have imagined. Frankly, I don't understand it." Paul needs to understand the reasons behind the numbers. He is also giving Terry an opportunity to explain that his plan is superior to others and, therefore, it costs a little more.

"I thought I explained all of that. You know, Dick Henderson over at Babcock-Schwaller thinks this is one of the best pricing packages to come down the pike in a long time. Do you know Dick?" Terry apparently doesn't realize that Paul expects a specific answer to his question and not general and friendly personal testimonials.

Paul is not very comfortable with Terry's overly casual manner. He is not relationship oriented when it comes to getting the job done. "Uh, well yes, slightly."

Terry interrupts him. He does not appear to be listening to Paul's concerns. "Well, like I said earlier, Paul, companies are going with a cafeteria approach to benefits. You know, employees take what appeals to them. Now that way you don't have to provide an expensive blanket."

"Yes, I understand that. But what I can't quite grasp is how this rate scale applies to all these combinations. It seems confusing." Since he sees that he's not getting through to Terry, Paul tries to be more specific in his request for information about the plan.

Terry does not seem to be prepared to answer this question. "Oh, we can work that out. You know, Paul, employees really don't want to know all the details. This is a very effective plan. People love it. Now any other questions?"

Love probably doesn't figure into Paul's need for cost analysis. He senses that Terry would like to close the sale. "Well . . ."

Terry becomes more aggressive. "You agree that you have a need for a policy like this?"

"Yes, but I'm still not comfortable with it." In his view, he has had little or no explanation of what the plan is.

"Oh? Why?"

"I don't see enough evidence that you've done an in-depth analysis of our company to determine all the possibilities. And I don't understand the schedule." He cannot make a decision without seeing how all the facts relate to his specific situation.

"It's really not that complicated. . . . Uh, Beth Sargent! I'll have her give you a call. She's got our plan over at Beacon."

After trying to make his point several times, Paul begins to avoid the issue. He does not want his staff's love or testimonials about how similar plans work at other companies right now. He'd just like to have the facts about the benefit package. "I'm sure it's fine for them."

"Paul, believe me, this is a great plan." Terry has not given Paul the information he needs to support this enthusiastic claim.

"That's not the point."

"It's one of the best in the industry. We're really proud of it." Still, he gives no facts to explain why it's one of the best, and he offers no indication that he might give more information in the future.

Paul looks at the quote for the plan. He sees no explanation there to answer his questions. "I'm sure, but I'd like a few days to think it over. You know, take the time to study your recommendations more thoroughly and share them with a few of the others. Leave me this policy quote, and the proposal. I'm sorry, Terry, I really don't have much more time to talk about it right now."

Terry is surprised by the abrupt end to the sales call. He doesn't understand what went wrong. He thought that he was on his way to a purchase agreement.

This did not have to be a lost sale. Even if Terry was unable to answer Paul's questions, he could have offered to have a cost analysis done for him by his own staff. He could have brought in to a meeting with Paul someone from his company's financial department to discuss matters in detail that Terry did not know or found uncomfortable to discuss.

The Ask-Assertive Analytical is easy to work with if you take the time to understand his needs and then offer him your proposal in detail. As long as you're prepared to answer his need for more facts and know that the sales process might be a long one, you should have no problem in dealing with this buyer. You will just have to take the initiative to keep the process moving. You may find that *you* will learn more about your product or service in your sales relationship with him. This can certainly be a benefit for you. See Exhibit 2 for a summary of the traits shown by the Analytical buyer.

An Analytical buyer is perceived as detail-oriented, deliberate, and well organized. This type of buyer listens and studies information carefully before weighing all alternatives with reference to established policies, criteria, and objectives. An Analytical buyer tends to avoid personal involvement with salespeople and lets others take the social initiative. In general, this type of buyer prefers an efficient, businesslike sales approach.

The Analytical buyer wants to understand the whole picture as opposed to the big picture. An Analytical's needs are best met when information is gathered in a systematic, efficient manner; sufficient information about the company, product, and service is provided; and time for processing recommendations is allowed.

Some phrases used to describe Analytical buyers are:

- Conservative and practical in business decisions
- Technically oriented; relies on structured approach and factual evidence
- Tends to avoid uncomfortable situations by changing the topic or withdrawing
- Prefers systematic, thorough approach to data-gathering and presentation of recommendations

The strengths commonly attributed to Analytical buyers include:

- Assures that company's needs are met
- Is careful about committing company resources
- Analyzes facts and evidence before deciding
- Makes practical, cost-effective buying decisions
- Approaches salespeople with caution, avoiding personal involvement

Exhibit 2   Summary of the Analytical Buyer

In Chapter 4, we'll take a look at the other Control-Responsive social style, the Driver. We'll see that the Driver is more interested in the big picture than the detail-oriented Analytical. He is also more direct in telling the salesperson just what he thinks.

4

The Driver: "Show Me I Can Get Some Bottom-Line Results"

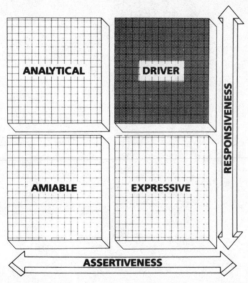

"I never could understand why people said I intimidated them. Also, it seemed that I wasn't thought of as especially versatile. This surprised me. It puzzled me because I certainly didn't intend to intimidate anyone. And even if I did, as a petite blond, I wouldn't have thought that that kind of aggressive behavior would have worked. Some of my confusion was cleared up when I found out that I was seen as an Expressive-Driver. I took a close look at my behavior and figured out why I was perceived as an intimidating person." This sales rep has since learned to use this knowledge in her favor to help her work with clients as well as her staff. She's a more effective salesperson and manager for it.

On the matrix, Drivers are shown as Control-Responsive and Tell-Assertive (Exhibit 1). Even though they can be pleasant in their relationships, on the whole, their responsiveness is seen as much more task than relationship oriented. In this regard, they are similar to Analyticals. Drivers are, however, much more assertive.

Don't be surprised if, after many meetings with a Driver client, the personal relationship that you thought you had so carefully nurtured didn't exist in the first place. Drivers are not the easiest people to get through to on a personal level. Not only that, it's a good bet that they don't necessarily expect you to be friendly. This isn't to say that the Driver can't be charming. As long as you play by his rules he can be delightful. Your shock comes if you have somehow not fulfilled his

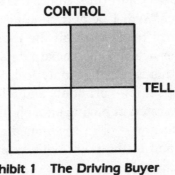

CONTROL

TELL

Exhibit 1   The Driving Buyer

performance expectations or if you somehow challenge his need for control.

"Relationship! What relationship? I don't want to burst your bubble, but you'd better get me some hard evidence that your equipment can do the job and then be able to convince me that your models have some long-range benefits."

None of the friendly Amiable personality here. If you are looking for clues from body language, although he'll be cordial, the Driver probably won't be one to give away too much of his inner thoughts and feelings in outward gestures or expressions. Actually, you might think that some Drivers are rather dead-pan. They are apt to be very businesslike and to the point. In the sales situation, you are expected to be the same. Glib friendliness won't work with the Driver client. It may give him the impression that you are too frivolous and therefore not to be taken seriously. There's a good chance that this initial impression you give could ruin your chance for success before you get very far along in the sales process.

Of course, he or she knows that you are a salesperson, but you've got to look and act the part of the businessperson, too. "I like salespeople who are properly dressed, who step up to bat; who stick to the point." Reasonable advice from the Driver.

Before you meet with the Driver client, ask yourself: "Do I have a businesslike attitude? Do I look like a businessperson? How can I find out this client's need most efficiently? Will I be able to isolate his particular problem and suggest the right solution(s) to help him? Can I offer him more options to allow him to make decisions? Will I be able to adjust my presentation to his schedule? Am I ready with all the performance figures on my product or service and the backup data if needed?"

Facts? No, this is not the Analytical. While the Analytical is interested in specifics—printouts and all—to mull over later, the Driver is interested in having enough information to get the overall view right now—or in the immediate future. Your facts should be clear and to-the-point with applications directed toward his needs.

Brett is selling office equipment to a small public relations service. The owner of the company, Ms. Doyle, is dressed in a designer gray suit. He knows that the recent growth of her company has been attributed to her aggressive push to get known in the community. Her photo is in the newspaper occasionally. She's able to find the time to work on the boards of various community organizations.

She's cordial, but somewhat brisk in her movements and glances at papers on her desk in a way that causes him to sense that perhaps she's anxious about a project. Most of her furniture appears to be highly polished oak; her accessories—file cabinets, paper bins, etc.—are gray and mauve. All are conservatively up-to-date in the latest models. She may have spent too much for some of her equipment in the beginning, but it seems to show a vision of what her goals are—to develop her business into a large public relations agency.

Now that she's expanding and needs more equipment, Brett feels that she should have a look at his full line. This way, she can get an idea of how she can buy now and add on later. After telling her his usual information about his company's manufacturing quality, he goes on to show her his equipment catalog. He goes over sizes, colors, expansion possibilities, and quality considerations.

Brett is so involved in his presentation that he hasn't noticed that by now she is not just glancing at her papers, but she is actually reading a report. She says, "Excuse me," and makes a phone call. During that time, he takes out his display of office set-ups and his company's new delivery schedule. Then she tells him that she's got to meet with a client, thanks him for stopping in, and asks him to leave some information for her to look over. She'll get back to him when she's ready to order gray letter-size file cabinets.

Ms. Doyle, like other Drivers, can easily become bored and impatient with details that are irrelevant to her. She might also have problems with listening to too much historical background information about your product or company. At the same time, your speculation—what she may see as fictional or overenthusiastic claims—about what your service or product will do for her in the future could be of little concern to her now. She wants practical options, not science fiction.

What this buyer wants to know is how whatever it is you are selling will help solve her problems most effectively right now. She sees it as your function to give her immediately useful information and recommendations that will help propel her to her own goals. Little details, for her, get in the way of her broad actions. She will usually give your printouts to others on her staff to decipher or read them later—if time allows.

The lumber and building materials company that Jack works for is anxious to get a contract with Tucker & Associates, the developer of the new mall in town. Jack and his staff have researched as fully as possible the plans for the mall. It will include a large department store, ten smaller store units, and a restaurant. Rumor has it that Tucker is looking for another mall site in a nearby town. Getting this contract could mean a lot to the future of Jack's company. It is his responsibility to pull it off.

Jack meets Tucker, a reserved but smiling man with graying hair, in his trailer office on the lot where the new mall will be built. The lot looks very large to Jack. He begins to get visions of how much income this project could give him. Tucker shows him the architect's plans and quickly points out which areas he thinks will need what types of building materials. He gives Jack the architect's other technical specifications.

Whatever the technicalities, it's become clear to Jack that his company's research missed the mark. There is a much larger need here than he'd expected. Meanwhile, Tucker seems to be enjoying having Jack listen to his great plans. Then he asks, "Can your company meet my requirements?"

"Our company can supply you with everything you need." Well, actually, it can but . . .

"Here's our schedule. Maybe you should look it over with your people and let me know how it fits."

Jack skims it and, although it appears too tight, he says, "You're right, I should talk it over with them, but it really looks fine with me."

His smile begins to look cynical. "Oh, really. You know, yesterday I spoke with a guy from Crown Lumber. He told me that in this area the supply of the quality lumber I need is pretty low. That waiting time could be up to six months for some of it. We've got stores already wanting to sign leases. I want the doors to this mall open in a year-and-a-half. Come back when you have a plan for me as to how you intend to supply us."

Jack packs up and leaves, thinking that Tucker's schedule is completely unreasonable. Maybe, though, he can get the suppliers to push things a little . . .

Ask-Assertive people may see Drivers as so aggressive about meeting goals that they lose track of the small practical facts that can make or break a project. However, just because the Driver is more interested in the end result than each minute detail, doesn't mean that you shouldn't have all the details *you* need at hand.

The Driver can be very fast at asking questions that relate to the bottom line and you'd better have the answers. He may really need to know something in order to help in decision making. However, the Driver's questions may be, in fact, his way of personally challenging you in order to maintain his own sense of power. If you cannot come up with helpful facts, you might lose credibility in the Driver's eyes. Remember, though, that if you harp on about irrelevant information you'll probably lose his interest.

Susan is a new financial services representative. She spends part of her time "cold calling" people on the phone in order to create interest and set up appointments. The rest of her time is spent calling on potential clients at home or at their offices.

She meets Mr. and Mrs. Rainer at their home. Mrs. Rainer retreats quietly to make coffee for the three of them, while Mr. Rainer listens intently to Susan's presentation, almost too intently—his eyes flash constantly every time she flips to a new display page.

He provides her with the basic information she needs— how much he wants to invest, how much risk is he willing to take, what kind of return he wants, and so forth. With each answer, his smile becomes more and more of a smirk. At any rate, he does seem interested, as she begins to present a recommendation on mutual funds.

Just as she gets to her final page, he blurts out, "And why should I buy from you when I could get a similar mutual fund from a no-load broker?"

"Because my company provides you with a service."

"What service is that? Telling me everything I already know about investing?"

"We keep a record of your account on our computer so that you always have the status of your transactions accessible."

He is interested in this. Susan tells him more of the services that her company provides. He says that he's interested but would like to think about the investment for a few days. Susan leaves him with brochures explaining in more detail what she just explained. He calls her the next day—ready to invest.

There are times when you will have to go into detail about your product or service. In this case, it is useful to have your information in writing. If the buyer does not ask for it earlier, after your presentation and discussion of the benefits of his working with your company, leave this written material for him to look over in his own time. You are giving him the space to work alone—something he enjoys.

With the practical-minded Driver, it is best to keep in mind "The Big Picture." Remember when Analytical Ben Cavett tried to pin down Driver Liz Donahue with the details of Liz's problems with his word processing system? To Ben, the system was installed five-and-a-half weeks ago; to Liz, it was an easy six weeks. Ben wanted to look at the service document to see exactly when service calls occurred. Liz only knew that there were too many of them. Ben wanted to know about user instruction; Liz thought this was a waste of time.

And, from her view it was. She just wanted the equipment fixed. It was of no consequence to her to know exactly when the system was installed. The fact is, as she sees it, it does not work now. It would be missing the point to think that she wanted to know the facts for historical perspective. History will not help her solve her problem. She wanted results yesterday. Today is almost too late.

Time is definitely an important factor for the goal-oriented Driver. Don't waste his, and he'll do his best not to waste yours. This should work if you are prompt and able to get to the point of your call as soon as possible. Easier said than done, you say? This can entail major adjustments in your presentation—but it just might be worthwhile it if you want a working sales relationship with this client.

> Jason is a friendly space salesperson who tries to get businesses to advertise in the magazine of the local arts complex. He very much enjoys working, even indirectly, with artists and performers. He is especially excited about the new theater production of a play by a local writer. It seems, though, that the more excited he is, the lower his sales numbers go. This is crucial because this particular performance needs local support.
>
> Before starting his presentation in the back office of Dave's computer store, Jason enthusiastically describes how well the rehearsals are going for this new show and how fantastic the lead actress is.
>
> Dave sees that Jason is settling in for a long visit. He asks for Jason's rate card and tells him that he'll send in his ad tomorrow if the price is right. Jason is not sure that Dave understands the excellence of the show. Also, he wants to take more time to get to know Dave, to build a relationship so that it will be easier to call on him in the future. Dave is already off showing a customer a new computer.

Driver clients do not want you to waste their time with extraneous facts or time-consuming chattiness. On the other hand, if you're the Driver, try not to be inflexible about your own schedule. It's OK for you to make allowances for sales calls that go overtime—especially if it means you'll get the sale. You might also want to take some time if the client seems to need more relationship building than you would normally provide.

A Driver salesperson says that he "used to get very tense if a call went over his allotted hour. Now that I'm a little more relaxed about time, I don't mind if the meeting goes a bit over my schedule. I've noticed that my customers seem to be more at ease and willing to buy." You can try this yourself. If you have to count to ten to keep your impatience under control, then do it.

The Driver client, though, wants to save time. The middle-manager Driver buyer has meetings to attend, a staff to manage, strategies to formulate. You fit in his scheme of things only by giving him the most efficient means of streamlining his operation. You are not there to shoot the breeze about the wonderful view from his office window.

It's almost too easy to say "Be prepared." In this case, though, we mean it. It's not enough to know your own company's product or service. The Driver expects you to fully understand *his* company as well.

Drivers are sometimes seen as pushy. This is great for getting a job done, but if you are, say, an Amiable salesperson, it might be just a bit more than you'd normally want to face—if you had a choice. Top this with his controlled outward responses, and you might feel as if you're dealing with the force and behavior of a brick wall. Behind this customer's wall he has a task goal and the only way that you can work with him is to respect its strength.

For you, listening is a good skill to have in dealing with Drivers. Since you might not get much information from body language, listen to what the Driver customer has to say about his or her company's problems and needs and go from there. For respecting him or her in this way, you will gain this customer's appreciation and respect.

An important point to keep in mind is that the Driver wants to maintain a semblance of being independent. This customer is not overly interested in being a team player. He is reasonably confident that he can manage and make decisions on his own, without constantly discussing the issues with his staff. He may even see this decision-making ability as the reward that's due him for having attained his position.

This is not like the Amiable who needs assurance from others that his decisions are OK, or who might even need the emotional cushion of a staff-originated decision instead of his individual one. The Driver—for good or ill—takes on the responsibility of leadership, preferably alone.

When the Driver does meet with a group, you might suspect that he has already made up his mind before the group meets, or that he will decide independently later. Since the Driver also needs to be in control, his decision may have a strong impact on the other group members. Naturally, it would be to your advantage to positively influence his decision.

Part of your job includes offering the Driver choices. Most Driver buyers do not like to be given only one possibility. He needs options to exercise his decision-making power. It is important that your choices be quite reasonable or else he may perceive a problem in your offerings. Back up each possibility with reasons why each could work in making his operation more efficient.

And then respond to what he has to say about your proposals. Your favorite one or two may be important to you, but they may have no or little value to him. You'll get further with him by simply letting him know the benefits of each option. Listen, suggest, but don't push.

There are times when a Driver's charm—as businesslike as it may be—may tempt you to let your guard down. You may think that he is really being friendly. Let's take a look at some of the mistakes a salesperson can make with a seemingly gracious Driver client.

John Carty is an Amiable salesperson in his early forties. He dresses in an appropriate businesslike manner. John is on his way to closing a deal with his client Peter Lockran, a Driver in his late forties. Peter has invited John to fly with him in the company plane to see the plant.

They're already in the plane waiting for take-off. John is holding a note pad with writing on it and seems to be prepared for business sometime, but not quite yet. He's enjoying the experience of his pleasant surroundings. Peter takes a minute to look up from the report that he's been reading to give John an idea of what the schedule will be. As usual, time is of the essence to this Driver and he intends to use this short trip for business. That is why he invited John along in the first place.

"We have a shuttle bus, but this way we'll be down and back before lunch. I've got an operations meeting at 2." He gives the impression that this is not meant to be a pleasant minivacation.

"Nice aircraft, Peter." John continues to look around almost as if he hadn't heard Peter.

"Yeah." Peter is getting anxious about the delayed takeoff. He asks on the intercom, "What's the hold, Harry. Problems? All right." Then he turns to Peter with his folder of reports. "Like I said, John, production costs are way too high. Gotta get them down. I need the right equipment." John thinks that since there is a delay he may as well use the time productively.

"Right. I understand. This is comfortable. Company had it long?"

"Huh? Yeah, a couple of years, I guess. Yeah, it's a good craft. Do you have that product information that I asked for so I can read it?" Peter thinks that even though John is enjoying himself, the salesperson can at least give him what he wanted so he can get started reviewing the equipment.

"Well, I thought we could go over that once we got back. You know, Peter, I appreciate your letting me come along on this inspection. Sort of fills in the picture, especially after seeing the plant. Gives me a better idea of your needs." Apparently, John doesn't realize that Peter sees this flight as a segment of the business trip. He also misses the point that Peter, as a Driver, needs to see solid facts.

"Yeah, well, it's important that I get a clear idea of exactly what your equipment can do."

John acts as if this were the opening he was looking for. "Well, like I've been saying all along, we've got the right configurations for you." Without bothering to mention what these configurations might be, he takes a piece of blank paper from his pocket. "Now, when we get to the plant, would it be all right if I talked to some of your people?" He prepares to list names on the paper.

"About what?" Peter doesn't understand why this Amiable salesperson would be interested in people at the plant.

"Don't you think we need to fill in the whole picture?"

Peter is becoming clearly irritated. "Like what?"

John is chatty and getting comfortable and relaxed in his seat. "Well, see how they feel about change-over, realignment, training . . ."

"Who cares? I've got a change-over schedule. What I don't have is a clear idea of what exactly your equipment can do." Peter is becoming annoyed with John's vague approach to the specifics of his company's equipment.

John is cheerful and friendly. "Well, believe me, when I say you should go with our equipment it's because I think our line is the best."

Peter is stunned by John's attitude—overblown in praise to his company, yet sadly lacking in facts. "And that is supposed to convince me?"

"Don't you think you can trust me on this? Now, we've spent a lot of time and energy developing this relationship." John is settled into his comfortable seat. He trusts his feelings about this sales relationship.

Peter is obviously angry. He leans forward and looks directly at John. "Relationship? What relationship? I don't want to burst your bubble, John, but you'd better get me some hard evidence that your equipment can do the job, and then be able to convince me that your models have some long-range benefits. Show me that I can get some bottom-line results." He abruptly opens his papers and starts to read.

John is confused, anxious, and hurt. He has nothing to offer in response. Even if he can come up with an acceptable sales strategy, it will be a long road back to gaining Peter's confidence.

John has clearly made mistakes in dealing with a Driver. John's Amiable need for personal relationships in the sales situation is of no consequence to Peter. This Driver client isn't especially interested in running John's numbers—if he has any—though his computer. He'd just like to skim some product information to assure himself that the equipment can do the job. John would have been able to enjoy the rest of the flight if he had just given this material to Peter. Peter's need to use this time to work would have been satisfied.

What John needed to know is that, as with all social styles, Drivers have their preferences and expectations in the way they do business. If John is to be more productive in this situation, he should learn to adapt to Peter's needs, to be more versatile.

From his viewpoint, a Driver salesperson says, "I have to be careful not to run over Amiables, especially if the tension level is rising. When that happens, I tend to want to control the situation, and even though they may give in, they resent me for it.

"Sometimes I lose patience with Expressives, especially if they seem to me to be 'flowery'—somewhat excessive in the way they present themselves.

"Analyticals are the hardest for me to get along with. I look for the big picture; they give me details.

"And other Drivers I have to be careful with. I work with a lot of Drivers and sometimes the situation turns into a tug-of-war. This leads to bruised egos. Then none of them wants any part of the project, especially when each sees that he or she can't be in total control of it.

"There is a big advantage in working with Drivers. That is, that when things go well, they get the job done. They don't waste time in deciding who'll do it. They do it, and it's over. On to the next project."

Keep in mind when you approach the Driver buyer: He or she wants action. This buyer will not allow you to sit back after your presentation. You will have to quickly respond to his situation or else you won't have a chance at making the sale. If you do get it, and you don't follow through with the results that he expects, you just might find that you've lost the customer.

Ronnie wholesales gift items to mail-order catalog buyers. A foreign manufacturer of brass novelty items has been highly recommended to her by her sales manager. Ronnie is impressed by the quality of the samples and the good price.

The manufacturer has been in business for a few years and has a good record of keeping to a regular production schedule. If specific requirements are provided and sufficient quantities are ordered, he will make new novelty items to order for individual customers.

Ronnie remembers that her largest customer—a specialty mail-order house—has sometimes requested exclusive items.

The buyer, June, is very interested in ordering gift sets for the Christmas catalog. When the samples arrive, June gives the OK to Ronnie to put through the order.

The order comes in time, however, the quality isn't the same as that of the samples. Apparently, the manufacturer had subcontracted the work to a new company in order to keep to schedule. June deletes the gift sets from her catalog and replaces them with other items from a wholesaler she considers to be more reliable than Ronnie.

As a Tell-Assertive Control-Responsive buyer, the Driver may appear to you as a solitary hard worker who wants to get

---

A Driver buyer is seen as controlling, forceful, and results-oriented. This type of buyer usually has clear objectives to achieve and responds to those who can demonstrate that their product or service can efficiently and effectively achieve results. A Driver tends to have a high sense of urgency and little need for establishing relationships with salespeople. This type of buyer wants to know options and their probabilities of success.

The Driver buyer wants a salesperson to listen carefully before recommending products and services. A Driver's needs are best met when information is gathered in an organized manner; the salesperson listens willingly and avoids becoming defensive; follow-up on requests is timely; case histories, references, and factual support are provided; and time for considering options is allowed.

Some phrases used to describe Driver buyers are:

- Knowledgeable and controlling in business decisions
- Goal-oriented; relies on information that supports results
- Tends to act quickly and confront issues directly
- Expects people to listen carefully and respond in a timely manner

The strengths commonly attributed to Driver buyers include:

- Keeps discussion focused on objectives
- Explains situation so that salesperson can recommend appropriate solution
- Makes expectations clear
- Acts quickly, after careful consideration of options
- Attempts to balance quality and cost considerations when making decisions

Exhibit 2   Summary of the Driver Buyer

the job done. You, the salesperson, should have a clear understanding of what the Driver needs.

Once you come up with a fit, a solution based on your company's products or services, the Driver might actually look forward to talking with you. He will see you as a possible means to fulfilling his need for results.

This fit usually has efficiency at its core. Its benefit to him is the practicality of what it will do. If he sees this product or service as an extension of his sense of power, he will buy—and he will expect what he has bought to do exactly what you said it would. See Exhibit 2 for a summary of Driver buyer traits.

In Chapter 5, we take a look at the Expressive buyer. This is the other Tell-Assertive social style, but the unlike the task-oriented Driver, the Expressive is more interested in personal relationships.

5

The Expressive: "I Like Salespeople Who Are Competent, Imaginative"

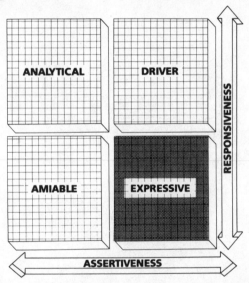

"I enjoy being a salesperson. I usually like working with customers—unless they become too picky about facts and numbers. I sell a good product that I like telling people about. But sometimes that can be a problem. I can overdo things, get too enthusiastic. So sometimes I've got to remember to go slower and tone things down, especially with my conservative buyers." This Expressive salesperson has learned to be versatile with his customers.

T he fast-paced Expressive is represented in the Tell-Assertive and Emote-Responsive quadrant (Exhibit 1). This client can be perceived as being more responsive than the Driver, more assertive and open than the Analytical, and more assertive than the Amiable. This buyer likes to work with people in a dynamic and creative environment. Although he enjoys thinking of himself as the leader in the sales relationship, he will expect the salesperson to be just as energetic as he is.

Gary sells imported fabrics to clothing manufacturers. Fortunately, he has some background in fashion design because most often he finds himself dealing with the designers themselves—especially when he calls on the smaller manufacturers, such as Lisa's firm.

Lisa, a children's clothing designer, makes a point of being

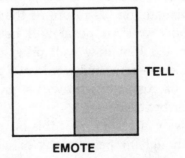

EMOTE

Exhibit 1   The Expressive Buyer

involved in buying the fabrics when she is in the process of designing a new line. She is usually very energetic and sometimes he has seen her having fun with the active, amusing toddler-size models.

Lisa does know what she wants. This becomes clear when she shows Gary some of the sketches for her new line. She, however, needs his input as to what fabrics are available and what can be made to her specifications. She fully expects Gary to be able to visualize the finished garments and to help her to adapt her designs according to the fabric possibilities.

This does not mean that she will always buy from him—there are times she just doesn't think that his fabrics are suitable. However, she enjoys working with him in the sales relationship because he's willing to use his imagination, just like most of her staff members. He is also willing to special order fabrics of her own design. She is usually anxious to order most of her fabrics from Gary.

Expressives can be good idea people. They can come up with a lot of ideas—the main problem can be that they have a hard time narrowing them down to one good idea. When they do, they tend to be very enthusiastic when they feel positive about an idea or project—and they want to spread their enthusiasm. This client especially enjoys working with people and getting others involved in seeing how an idea can become a reality. He or she can be very cooperative with you if you are able to show how your product or service can help along these lines.

Don't be afraid to use your imagination. This customer expects it. Try visualizing his future as the Expressive sees it. That is, show how your proposal will help him realize his dreams. You can tell him how well other clients—especially mutual acqaintances—benefited from your product or service. The Expressive is a customer who will appreciate personal referrals from other buyers.

Of course, we can assume that this buyer is in a responsible position. Although he bases many of his decisions on his intuition, he does like to know the facts behind your proposal.

The Expressive is a big picture person. He does not want to discuss all the details. He knows that he needs some facts—and expects you to supply them—but too many facts will make him restless. If you try to discuss too many details, you may lose his interest—and the sale. Get the facts down on paper. This way, the client can read whatever he chooses to know of the facts after your meeting.

> Bruce is a personnel agency manager who was given the task of finding an appropriate telephone system for the office. He has skimmed some information sent to him by several companies, but what he really wants to do is discuss the systems. So, when Cal calls him he was ready to talk.
>
> The system that Cal can offer him is fairly standard. It is an adequate system at a reasonable price. When he gives his presentation in the comfortably furnished contemporary conference room at Bruce's agency, he highlights the technical dependability of this kind of system. That is, until Bruce interrupts him before he's half finished.
>
> Bruce is not especially interested in the technicalities. He'd just like to know what the system can do. Cal understands that, but he says that it would be difficult to know what the system can do without understanding the technical aspects of the equipment.
>
> After a few more minutes of this presentation, Bruce cannot contain his restlessness. He asks Cal for references of people who have actually used the system. He'd like to call them to find out how the system works. Cal tells him that his customers have been very pleased with the cost and dependability of the system, however, he does not give Bruce any names of customers. Instead, he gets back to his place in his presentation.
>
> Bruce interrupts him again. He asks Cal to leave information about the system, and tells him that he'll have to get back to him because he is pressed for time. After Cal leaves, Bruce glances at the system information and tosses it away. He calls another company.

During your sales call, if he is interested in your offer, the Expressive will probably want to use the time brainstorming. He may take your basic facts in highly original directions that you hadn't considered. His thinking can be very innovative and creative. And he will expect you to be able to keep up with the fast pace of his ideas.

Go with it to the degree that it helps define what it is that this customer really wants from your product or service. However, it is best not to let the discussion get too far afield. You may have to pull in the reins, at times, just to keep the conversation on track. You may also have to remind him of the basic facts if his imagination really does go too far afield.

Betty has just bought a chain of family restaurants that are in the downtown areas of several cities. She wants to redecorate to give them a more contemporary look. She meets Allen, a salesperson for a restaurant furnishings supplier, at one of the restaurants. Allen is very knowledgable about restaurant design. Both of them thought that actually being at one of the locations would make it easier to visualize just what it is that Betty wants.

Almost as soon as they meet, Betty shows Allen color cards that respresent a color scheme of earth tones—tan, orange, brown—that she would like to use as a base for decorating. She thinks that these colors are appropriate for her family-style restaurants. She also indicates that she wants moderately priced furnishings.

Allen shows her his catalog of this line of furnishings. She looks through it anxiously. Finally, however, she doesn't think that this line is "classy" enough.

She asks to see another catalog that he has in his case. This one is more exciting for her—more expensive, too. She especially likes one series of items that is in the colors gray, mauve, and white.

She tells him that this is the color scheme that she has in her home. Allen is not sure that this is really what she wants for her moderate fare, family-style restaurants. Besides, he thinks that the total cost of everything that she would need would be beyond her limits.

He doesn't bring this up, however. Instead, he casually mentions that although she has good taste in her home furnishings, she might better serve the needs of her restaurants by going with her original idea. At any rate, he tells her that the decision is up to her.

>To help her along, he shows her photos of how other restaurants have been set up using the earthtone colors. She does find some of them appealing and is ready to go back to her own plans. They go back to look at the first catalog and discuss her design ideas. Allen feels that he is on course to a purchase agreement.

You will find in your discussions that, unlike the Amiable (the other Emote-Responsive social style), the Expressive usually doesn't mind taking a risk. He truly believes in his own idea. If he can find the means to see it through, he will take the lead in getting his innovative idea to become an actual fact. In varying degrees, he is willing to take risks to achieve his goal.

Since he likes working with people, he expects you to become a member of his team to help get his project going. His outgoing, friendly style can be a strong motivator in encouraging others to take part in the progress. One way that he achieves this is by establishing open, trusting relationships with his coworkers, salespeople, and anyone else who can help him to reach his goals. He is then able to use the positive aspects of these relationships to keep his team working.

In this situation, he may want to be the leader. At the least, he will want to be recognized for the value of his ideas. Those who work with him, including salespeople, should understand this. With the Expressive in a leadership position, it would be a mistake to attempt to force on him your own views and facts. He expects others to know that he is in control and that their roles provide a means for him to realize his vision. As long as you take care of your role, you'll have a very friendly relationship with him.

>Max sells cardboard cartons to manufacturers. He considers himself to be something of an expert in his work. He knows everything from the qualities of the trees to how they're made into cartons according to the manufacturers' specifications. Although he knows all this, he does not feel the need to overwhelm his customers with this information.

Hank is a buyer for a large appliance manufacturer. He needs a new supplier for cartons. His previous supplier started out fine, but then began to give Hank inferior quality cartons for the same cost. From what he's heard, Max's company supplies good quality cartons for a reasonable price so he's willing to meet with Max.

As far as Hank is concerned, he knows what he wants and he thinks that Max can supply this. What he's got to be sure of is that he and Max can get along in a friendly and trusting sales relationship over an extended period.

Throughout his presentation, Max questions Hank about his needs and allows Hank to speak at length about them. When Hank wants to bring up a point, Max listens. He offers Hank suggestions based on his expertise. Hank is impressed and sees Max as a valuable resource.

Max offers Hank the names of buyers at several other large manufacturers as references. Hank does call a few of them and, as he expected, the reports are good. He has positive feelings about working with Max.

If you try to be the leader, you may be in for a bit of verbal attack from the Expressive buyer. He can be surprisingly quick with this if he feels that your details—or even your own ideas—are getting in the way of his thoughts. He will not mind discussing your facts, as long as they relate to his big picture. However, he will want you to realize that the details are not necessarily valuable in themselves. They become useful only when they contribute to his goals.

Salespeople of other social styles, especially Analyticals, may have a difficult time adjusting to the Expressive's creative interpretation of the facts as well as his rather direct verbal style. Do not be surprised if this client tells it like it is no matter how uncomfortable the situation may be. If he has a problem with some aspects of your proposal, you can be sure that he will let you know.

Nat sells mutual fund packages. Many of his leads come from people who call his office after hearing an ad on the radio. Others respond by way of coupons in personal finance oriented magazines.

Chris, an Expressive customer, had heard the radio ad and called Nat's company because he had the general idea that mutual funds might be a way to save and increase some of his income—with the added bonus of a little stimulating risk.

When Nat calls on him at his home, Chris is very excited. This is the first time that he considered actually investing in something other than a savings account. He has prepared for Nat's visit by reading all the information that Nat's company sent him as well as discussing mutual funds with some of his friends who have invested. He has his checkbook at hand. He's anxious to get started.

Nat is prepared with his usual presentation. This includes a general discussion of the various packages, their benefits in particular, and a breakdown of costs and potential returns on the investment. Nat has his calculator ready to show examples that will back up his claims about returns.

When Nat is halfway through the presentation of low-risk funds, he notices that Chris is thumping his fingers on the table. Nat ignores this and continues his discussion. Chris interrupts him to say that he's not really interested in these funds. He asks about something that could give him a higher return, even though that would mean a higher risk.

Nat tells him that he'll get to those funds but first, he wants Chris to get the whole picture of all of his packages. With this knowledge, he feels that Chris will be able to pick and chose his investments more intelligently. Chris tells him again that he's not interested in the low-risk funds.

Nat believes that a more reasonable approach to investing for Chris would be to combine several funds—low-risk with the high-risk. Chris does not like Nat's attitude. He knows what he wants. He tells Nat that he just wants him to stop discussing details so that he can give him a check for the mutual funds that he chose himself, and then start watching his investment grow, he would hope.

This flusters Nat. He has gotten a sale, but somehow has lost the customer.

This can be even more devastating to a salesperson if the Expressive decides that he doesn't like something about the personal side of your sales relationship. This buyer isn't known for holding his tongue. If he feels pushed to it, he can be quite direct in his verbal attacks.

With this in mind, it would be best for you not to try to aggressively close the sale. The Expressive wants to be in control of making his own decision. He may work with others and respect what they can do for him, but he does not expect anyone else to decide for him what he needs. If you try to do this, you'll certainly hear about it, negatively.

You can influence his purchase by offering him the best quality solution to his problem that you can come up with. The Expressive is impressed by good quality products and services. What he feels about your proposal is more of a deciding factor for him than any analysis of the hard facts of the black-and-white bottom line. So, it is his personal feelings about the quality of your offer, as well as your personal sales relationship with him, that can get a positive response from this buyer.

When he has decided to make a purchase commitment, you can then back up his imaginative goals with your practical implementation plans. The Expressive isn't particularly interested in working out the final details. For this, he depends on you to follow through. Again, though, give him as much of the plan's overview that he needs—but don't overdo the details in your meeting with him. Instead, discuss an overview of the facts with him and, as for the finer details, give them to him in writing. This is what can happen if you become too assertive with facts.

> Tom Patrick, an Expressive manager in his late thirties, is moving his department into new offices due to expansion. Mary Sicotte, early thirties, is an Analytical salesperson of computer software. They are both walking in the holding area where Tom's department furnishings are temporarily stored. Mary is carrying a copy of her written proposal so that she can refer to it easily. Although he would like to see things move along faster, Tom is enthusiastic about his company's expansion.
>
> "And I think that should give us more room in this area. Well, this is our second expansion in three years. Now, don't get me wrong. It's great to be growing, but talk about

adjustments! I mean, look at this place. Now, we were supposed to move up to the eighth floor two weeks ago. And, well, here—we're still storing our office furniture down here. Quite a mess, isn't it?" Tom is friendly and easygoing. Sure, things are a mess right now but he sees the big picture—the expansion itself and what it will mean to his department.

"What about the inventory of VDTs. Where will they go?" Mary is interested in the details of the move.

"Uh, well, we'll be putting several of them along that wall. Like I said, we have to expand, but I'm concerned. There's so much software on the market today. This looks good; that looks good. It's hard to get a handle on it. I need to get in touch with some other users." Tom would like to have some personal referrals to get a better understanding of solutions to his problem.

"Well, that's what this proposal's for, Tom, to help you get the facts. You'll see that our software program has a 92 percent compatibility with your present hardware. The figures are based on a user network of thirty customers that we've been monitoring for three years." Instead of referring him to people, Mary refers him to the facts in her proposal.

Tom is interested. "Good. I want to get in touch with some of those customers." The Expressive heard only her mention of the customers in her study, not the numbers.

"Well, I have that information, but what's really vital here is the compatibility ratios that our product has achieved with various hardware." She pushes the proposal at Tom. "If you just look at the list on page two . . ."

Tom interrupts her. He is slightly annoyed that she is continuing with these technicalities, but he would like to clarify his needs. "Wait a minute, Mary. I don't want to look at numbers, not now. What I do want to do is find out who the users on the network are. I want to hear what they feel now about the way your software handles inventory control? What are they saying about time and effort?"

"Fine. Before we get to that, let's look at some of these functional details." The Analytical is persistent about dealing with details before going on to larger issues.

Tom is clearly getting irritated. "Hey. All I want to do is get a feeling for this stuff!"

"Right. I understand, Tom. But I think it's important to have a thorough understanding of this proposal before we make comparisons with other users." Mary does not understand

Tom's need to use his intuition, not logic, at this point in his decision-making process.

Tom has been pushed enough to attack. "Am I talking to a wall?! Now maybe you find those facts and figures interesting, but I don't, not now. I ask for apples, and you give me oranges. I'll read these figures when I'm ready. Now, if you can't tell me what I want to know, we're done talking!"

Mary will have to become more versatile than she's been up to this point or else her sales relationship with Tom will end abruptly. It would be to her advantage to allow him to contact the personal references that he needs. She can leave the proposal for him to read when he is ready.

An Expressive buyer is perceived as fast-paced, outgoing, and enthusiastic. This type of buyer often has a vision of the future and is responsive to products, services, and people that help achieve that vision. An Expressive will take the time to establish an open, trusting relationship with those who can make it easier to achieve goals. This type of buyer wants a salesperson to collaborate in finding and implementing quality solutions to meet needs.

The Expressive buyer wants to see the "big picture" before probing the details. An Expressive's needs are best met when the salesperson questions and listens well, can demonstrate competence, allows buyer input to the proposal, helps the buyer obtain internal support for the proposal, and stays on top of the implementation.

Some phrases used to describe Expressive buyers are:
- Futuristic, holistic in thinking
- Motivating; attempts to make others enthusiastic about visions and ideas
- Tends to be direct and open, even in uncomfortable situations
- Prefers collaborative, team approach to problem-solving

The strengths commonly attributed to Expressive buyers include:
- Openly offers information to help salesperson meet needs
- Collaborates on proposal to make it effective within the organization
- Concerned about the quality of solutions and their implementation
- Adaptable to the needs of others
- Innovative; willing to take risks

Exhibit 2   Summary of the Expressive Buyer

The Emote-Responsive Expressive can be very cooperative if his or her relationship needs are met. In that respect, this style is similar to the Amiable who we will discuss in the next chapter. See Exhibit 2 for a summary of Expressive buyer traits.

6

The Amiable: "Show Concern for Me and My Problems"

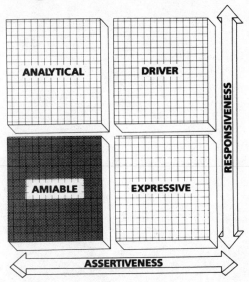

An Amiable salesperson says, "I like to meet my clients on a personal one-to-one basis. I don't want to appear overenthusiastic or brainwashed by my company's marketing information. I always look or ask for feedback from the customer. This helps develop rapport. If you let them know what you can personally do for them, it helps to build a trusting relationship. But most important is that I listen, listen, listen."

The Amiable buyer will show Ask-Assertive reserve combined with Emote-Responsive warmth (Exhibit 1). This buyer may appear to be more open than the Analytical and less aggressive than the Expressive. Because of these qualities, many salespeople see Amiable clients as good listeners. One way that this is evident is that the Amiable can be politely receptive to you.

Unlike some Tell-Assertives, this buyer will not try to aggressively take control of your presentation. Actually, they can be very cooperative because they enjoy working with others, salespeople included, if they feel that you can really help them get the job done or solve a problem.

Feelings—or just plain gut reactions—are very important with the Amiable. You've got to work with the Amiable buyer to create an atmosphere of friendly respect. Before they will even

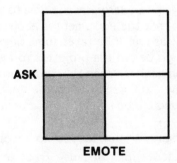

Exhibit 1   The Amiable Style

consider buying from you, they will have to trust you enough to work at—with much help from you—building a strong sales relationship with you.

> Jerry is a building contractor who has great rapport with his work crews. He's taken on a new project—renovating a landmark school into condos. His crew has needed new equipment for a long time but they haven't complained much to Jerry because they know that he does the best he can for them in other ways.
>
> He's very aware of their needs, however, and with this new contract this is as good a time as any to purchase new equipment. He asks Howard, a building equipment salesperson, to give him a call. Jerry has heard of Howard's company from another contractor friend of his. Howard, who wants to make sure of customer satisfaction with his equipment, has a good reputation of following through after the sale.
>
> Howard is a Driver salesperson who is very task-oriented. He gets right into discussing the precise equipment that Jerry needs for his new project. When Jerry comments on how his crew members have been patient about getting new equipment, Howard doesn't seem to hear him. Instead, he shows Jerry information on how his equipment is made and why it is of such high quality. When Jerry wants to take some time to show this to some of his workers, Howard starts talking about how this equipment can help Jerry keep his investment costs down.
>
> By the time Howard is finished with his presentation, Jerry is a little bewildered by all this. At this time he'd just like to be able to talk to his crew about the equipment, and then take a leisurely look at the cost figures.
>
> The next day, when Jerry has the time to review Howard's materials, he feels that the equipment is about average anyway so it might be just as well if he takes some time to look around. He has time enough before the project is to begin to get a feel for some other companies. When Howard phones, Jerry just tells him that the crew isn't happy with the equipment and they want to look around a little more.

As the salesperson, it's up to you to recognize the Amiable's relationship orientation, because trust and personal respect are high on the Amiable's list of priorities in their dealings with you. They want to know that you are sensitive to their needs. That you care enough about them to take time out from task goals to develop the personal aspects of the relationship. In other words, with Amiables, you may have to temper your businesslike approach with friendly concern for the customer's needs.

If you do this, and continue to provide a good product or service, there's a good chance that the Amiable will remain loyal, even in the face of competition. Of course, if the Amiable is already buying from the competition, then you have a tougher problem in getting him to break the former relationship. The Amiable may like the comfort of going to a salesperson he is used to even if his product is inferior to yours.

> Bob, an Expressive, carries a line of store displays that has been a good seller to store managers in small towns who want to modernize the look of their stores. He's been particularly successful in one town where the influx of new service industries has changed the feel of the town—from an easy rural area to a busy office workers' town.
>
> Most of the store owners have realized that in order to compete with the new mall, they have to update their stores. But then there's Ted, an Amiable. He owns a hardware store that has catered to a more agricultural market. He refuses to notice that much of the farm land now holds condos for the new workers. They go to what he calls the "hardware boutique" in the mall. He misses the friendly country style of those of his old customers who have left.
>
> Ted looks forward to his visits from the salesman who has "always been there" to replace broken shelves, racks, and so forth. He sees Bob as a brash city type who just wants to get him to renovate so that Bob can make a sale. Bob, on the other hand, has managed to be friendly toward Ted on his few calls at his store, although the store owner has tried his patience from time to time.
>
> On Bob's third visit to Ted's store, he notices that Ted is beginning to feel anxious about the future of his business. Ted tells him that he's too young to retire and is not interested in working for anyone else. Bob, having analyzed Ted as an Amiable, sees this as a way of starting to build a relationship with

Ted. Bob tells him how other store owners have been able to pull themselves out of this kind of slump. He gives Ted personal advice, unrelated to his sales display products, and tells Ted he will check on him next week.

The following week, Bob is surprised to get a friendly reception from Ted. Ted has actually looked over some of Bob's sales brochures that he had left there months ago. Ted wants to make a change and he wants Bob's help. Bob's on the way to a good sales relationship with Ted.

Driver and Analytical salespeople may get the impression that Amiables are more interested in people than the job at hand. That is, that the Amiable is more interested in how his staff will feel about a new product or service than he is in how this new product will help him achieve his task goals. For many Amiables, this may be true. This doesn't mean, however, that Amiables won't get the job done. Of course, they will—it's just that they go about doing the work in a friendlier, sometimes slower style.

Remember that this is the buyer who said: "I'm more receptive when salespeople are relaxed and able to show concern for me and my problems. I want that person to talk to me about my company. I want to know we can work together. Ask questions in detail. Information, and time to digest it, is important for both of us."

You will be disappointed if you expect the swift decision-making ability of the Driver here. Amiables are much more cautious. You may see them as highly competent people and then find yourself perplexed to hear that quite often they don't like making decisions by themselves. The Amiable buyer wants to be secure in knowing that his staff has taken part in choosing a product or service that will benefit everyone. Therefore, decisionmaking by committee is not unusual with this buyer. You may find yourself in the midst of discussions and more discussions with the Amiable buyer, his staff, and anyone else whose opinion the Amiable might want in relation to your proposal.

Louise works for a small audiocassette company. She is responsible for buying published materials that can be produced as cassettes. She has good knowledge of her field. The sales reports show that the cassette sales of the materials she's bought have been quite good.

Ron's publishing company has a new series of titles that would make fine cassettes. Both he and Louise know this, yet she is cautious about buying. In her view, those who work in production deserve some say in the buying process because they are the ones who will have to schedule and produce these new products. They also have to be able to understand what the product is.

Louise feels that it's definitely important for her own sales staff to know of the product before it is bought so that they can come up with ways of fitting the new products in the existing line, or come up with objections if this mesh will be impossible.

Since Bob has worked with Louise before, he is prepared this time. When the meeting with production and sales people is called, he brings in a few members of his own staff who are best suited to discuss any questions that Louise and her staff might come up with.

He leaves additional information with them because he knows that Louise's staff will continue the discussion informally during the next week. He also makes himself and his staff available to answer any questions that may arise before his final meeting with Louise.

This cooperative approach works for Bob in this case. However, he does not end the relationship when he sells Louise most of the titles in his new series. He continues to check with her to make sure that the production process is going well and that her sales staff has enough information. With this supportive attitude toward the sale, Bob will have an even easier time selling his next series to Louise.

The Amiable can be very concerned about getting input from his staff for several reasons. As with you, he has taken time to develop trusting relationships with those in his own organization. Since he probably has a stronger relationship with them than he does with you, he does not want to destroy that trust by purchasing something that will negatively affect them.

To some extent, he sees their concerns as being as important as his own. He does not want anything new that they will think of as worthless in solving their problems. He will request that they ask questions or add any information they may have that's pertinent to the purchasing decision.

Even if you do not have to participate in group discussions, you will be expected to be available to answer his staff's questions and, if necessary, to give them more information. The Amiable buyer wants to be as certain as possible that what you are offering will provide the best solution to his staff's problem. You will find that the Amiable can be very sensitive to the needs of others—even yours if the sales relationship has been positive.

You may begin to get the feeling that this buyer is making a mountain out of a molehill. That, in your view—especially if you are Tell-Assertive—what could have been a relatively simple decision for one person with the authority to make, has become a complex web of meetings and further discussions. You may see the deadline for a decision approaching while the Amiable continues with his friendly conversations.

Be patient. What this buyer really wants, before making a decision, is to be absolutely sure that whatever he decides will be fully accepted by his organization. He also wants assurance that you can be depended upon in keeping your commitments. In this sense, your relationship with him can be more important than your company's good reputation. After all, he and his staff are depending on you—personally.

Things can go very smoothly with the Amiable. Keep in mind, however, that if you do not go along with his style in the sales process, you may not build up the necessary relationship for him to make a purchase.

Steve is the production manager at a furniture factory. Lately, he has been getting a few complaints from his customers and workers about problems with the adhesive used in the manufacturing process. The supplier that he has depended on for the past four years has changed the formula for the adhesive and has not responded to his request for the old product, the one that worked well for him.

Reluctantly, he calls in Ed, a salesperson from another supplier. Ed gives him all the information he needs to make a decision based on his manufacturing specs. Ed leaves him with enough samples and the promise of a good discount to ease the decisionmaking process for Steve. As for Steve, he feels that Ed has left rather abruptly and wonders why he has not even taken the time to observe the manufacturing process in his plant. He doesn't think that Ed really knows what his workers need to improve the finished product.

Steve's task needs force him to continue considering Ed's company as a new supplier. Ed, however, is very difficult to reach when Steve wants to ask questions. His foreman, who has used some of the samples, is interested in asking Ed a few things too. Steve would like to set up a group meeting.

When Steve finally does contact him, Ed cannot come out to the plant to talk with him and his foreman because of scheduling problems. Instead, he sends Steve more sales materials. Steve does not know what to do but he has noticed that there are fewer complaints lately. Perhaps the adhesive they've been using isn't so bad after all. For now, he may as well continue to use it. He doesn't see any real alternative.

Simply providing your company's sales information and going to the Amiable's meetings will not be enough. You must work at developing trust with him and his staff. Without this step, you may notice that your Amiable buyer is quietly withdrawing. He may not respond directly to your questions or will not freely discuss his needs. His Emote-Responsiveness will seem to have been shut off. You will have a harder time getting any decision—positive or negative. In fact, you may be frustrated by the fact that the Amiable buyer simply won't communicate with you as freely as you would come to expect.

If you have not shown that you can be a friend first, then a dependable salesperson, the Amiable will not want to have much to do with you. Going through the motions of taking this buyer out to lunch or providing other amenities, does not always mean friendliness—especially if the lunch overly emphasizes the business aspects of your relationship. The Amiable expects more. Here is an example.

Barbara Fields is a rather businesslike Driver salesperson in her late thirties. She has had previous discussions with Karen Harris, an Amiable buyer in the communications field, about the possible purchase of a new word processing system. Barbara understands Karen's options and knows what system her company can provide to improve Karen's office operations. Since Barbara knows Karen's needs, to this salesperson, the choice is relatively simple.

The two women are at a restaurant where Barbara has invited Karen, who is about the same age as Barbara, to lunch. Barbara is anxious to get started with the business at hand. She gives Karen a product portfolio to read, while she prepares for a presentation with several other brochures on the table in front of her. They have not yet ordered lunch.

"So, Barbara, my main concern is how this new system will affect my people. Your 1200 BCD here is pretty sophisticated. It may be more than we need." The Amiable Karen does not mind discussing business—as long as her staff is taken into consideration.

"Karen, changeover is always a concern." Barbara does not relate this to Karen's specific concern. Actually, she brushes it aside as simply a small part of this total package.

"You know, Barb, I'd feel a lot better about this if I had a clearer picture of where the organization as a whole is coming from. How are you people able to bring all this new stuff together?" The Amiable would like to know more about the people behind the product. It is not enough for her to read brochures about the product and the company.

"Since January we've had a very aggressive market research program. It's given us a very clear idea on where this communication industry is going." Barbara is not describing the people in "the organization as a whole," she's discussing only a small part of it.

"Uh huh. You know, you couldn't have picked a better spot. They have a Salade Nicoise here that is out of this world." Karen would like to bring the conversation to a more personal level.

"Well, I hope you don't mind mixing business with your salad," says Barbara glancing at her menu but not ordering. Business is very obviously Barbara's priority.

"No. I like getting to know people outside the office." Karen would sincerely like to get to know Barbara and continues to try despite Barbara's businesslike approach.

"You bet. Now, Karen, what I what I want to talk to you about today are those terminals for the 1200. We're only carrying the discount three more days." Barbara is clearly the task-oriented Driver who does not understand Karen's need for relationship building.

"Mmmm hmmm." Karen fidgets as Barbara talks. This could be a sign that Karen is beginning to withdraw. Barbara has missed the opportunity to spend time relating with Karen in a friendlier, less businesslike, manner.

"Buying on discount is going to save you thousands of dollars." Barbara continues discussing the sale. She doesn't realize that it is her relationship with Karen and not necessarily the discount that will make or break this potential sale. To a Driver customer, the possibility of getting a discount as well as the perfect system could be a great incentive to deciding to buy now—not necessarily so with the Amiable.

"I . . . I understand that. And the discount is very attractive." Karen hands Barbara a menu. "Do you like seafood?" Karen assumes that part of the reason for meeting in the restaurant is to eat lunch.

"I love it. I just want to make sure that you understood our discount policy."

"I understand everything. I just need more time." Karen is beginning to retreat from the sales process. Amiables do not like to be pressured to make decisions.

"Time?"

Karen almost wants to express her dismay. She feels that Barbara is at fault for not knowing or caring enough to understand her needs. "Yes, time. I'm not convinced that you want . . . that is, that your new system is the best move. Not right now."

Barbara leans forward to further explain. "OK, OK, if you think the 1200 BCD is too sophisticated, we can always look at the 300."

Karen leans back a bit and holds her menu, like a shield, between herself and Barbara. "Maybe. The 300 seems right, too. I'm just not sure." She looks around for someone to give her lunch order to. "You know, it's funny. The service here is usually pretty good."

"Look, Karen, this is how I look at it. The sooner your
system is installed, the faster your branches will be able to start
talking to each other. And that's important in your business."

"Well, yes, of course. That's the whole idea." Karen sees
the *people* in the branches talking. She is not sure that Barbara
fully understands the significance of people talking.

"So, why don't we write up an order for the 1200 BCD.
You can take advantage of the discount, and get the system
you need." In addition to not sensing the relationship tension,
apparently she did not hear or want to discuss the possibility
that the 300 might be a better system for Karen's task needs.

"Well, I really want more time to think this over, but then
we'll miss the discount, won't we. Hmmm. It does seem to be the
system we need. All right. Why don't you write up the order—
there's no harm in doing that. Besides, if I change my mind, I can
always let you know." Karen goes along with Barbara's sugges-
tion to get herself out of an uncomfortable, pressured situation.

Barbara cannot be very certain that she actually got the
sale. There's a good possibility that Karen just might cancel
the order.

Patience, friendliness, and cooperation are some of the
points that Barbara hasn't expressed well enough in the sales
process to get a firm commitment from Karen. From Karen's
view, the Driver's style may also appear too pushy, too aggressive for an Amiable's comfort.

Karen, as with many Amiables, does not express herself
openly when working with someone she perceives to be as
aggressive as Barbara. Karen will sometimes understate her
feelings. This can cause problems for Amiable buyers in communicating with Tell-Assertive salespeople. Instead of saying
directly what she needs, the Amiable buyer might expect the
salesperson to already be aware of her needs.

In dealing with the Amiable buyer, you may have to allow
for more time in your initial presentation and subsequent sales
calls. This relationship building time can make the difference in
how the Amiable perceives meeting with you. He can see it either as a pleasant visit with a friendly salesperson who can help
him solve his and his staff's problems, or as an uncomfortably

tense appointment with a high-pressure salesperson who only succeeds in bombarding him with facts, numbers, and deadlines for discounts.

> Toni is the manager of a large bookstore. Although she took the position because she enjoys discussing books, she spends more time taking care of purchases and accounts than she does talking to customers. She really enjoys taking time out from her printouts to talk about the latest books with book distributor reps who usually seem to her to be a friendly group.
>
> Unfortunately, there is one—Dennis—who she really dreads seeing. Instead of discussing books he pulls out his own printouts to show her why she should buy certain titles. His company does offer good deals on display stands and other

---

An Amiable buyer is seen as warm, cooperative, and deliberate. This type of buyer generally gathers information and processes it with others before making a decision. An Amiable wants to establish a strong, trusting relationship with a salesperson prior to considering a purchase. This type of buyer wants to be assured that buying decisions will be supported by others and that the salesperson will keep commitments.

The Amiable buyer wants to feel assured that the product or service will be accepted. An Amiable's needs are best met when a trusting relationship is established and the salesperson takes time to understand the needs of the buyer and the organization and is very responsive to requests and problems.

Some phrases used to describe Amiable buyers are:

- Careful but cooperative in business situations
- People-oriented; relies on the support of others and shared decision-making
- Tends to avoid uncomfortable situations by withdrawing or changing the topic
- Prefers interactive approach to problem-solving

The strengths commonly attributed to Amiable buyers are:

- Assures that others will accept buying decisions
- Carefully determines whether commitments will be honored
- Processes recommendations with others before deciding
- Is sensitive to the needs of others in the buying process
- Establishes trusting relationships with others

Exhibit 2   Summary of the Amiable Buyer

helpful sales displays but he does not seem interested in helping her use or set them up.

Since some of his titles do go over well with her customers she usually does give him an order. However, she takes a minimum amount of time in going over his catalog and in placing orders. Sometimes this means that he gets a minimum order. Toni feels that this compensates for the negative feelings that she gets from him.

Given the best conditions, the Amiable buyer should be able—by his very nature—to get along with most salespeople. He can bring warmth to an Analytical's presentation of facts, personalize the Driver's task-oriented goals, and cooperate with the Expressive's people-oriented friendliness. See Exhibit 2 for a summary of the Amiable buyer's traits.

The versatile salesperson will use this knowledge to his or her advantage and not overwhelm the Amiable with Tell-Assertiveness or task orientation that could overwhelm the Amiable buyer. This will help keep the sales relationship in the productive-comfort zone. A discussion of what can happen if tension gets out of hand with Ask-Assertive Amiables and Analyticals is coming up in Chapter 7.

7

Ask-Assertive Backup Behavior: Flight

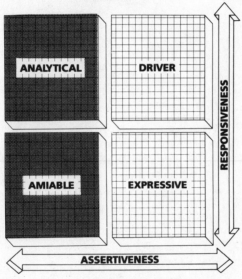

"It is important to maintain productive tension when you meet with your customers. This means that during your sales relationship with a client you balance relationship and task tension so that everyone is comfortable and concentrating on the job at hand and not distracted with unproductive tension."

It is the versatile salesperson's responsibility to maintain productive tension. You will have a head start on this if you know what the buyer's social style is.

We have already taken a look at the behavior of the four social styles, let's be more specific about how each style deals with tension. Each social style has its own pattern. Your ability to recognize and cope with each will ease many a tense situation, and probably save many a sale. This ability should help you with keeping your sales relationships on an even keel.

Tension in sales relationships cannot be avoided. Used productively, tension can have a positive effect on pushing the sales situation forward. The problem for you, the salesperson, comes when the tension is so high that the customer is saying in his own way, "I can't take this tension anymore." It's at this point that we say that the client has gone into the *backup behavior* that is appropriate for his social style. With some practice on your part, however, what may seem to you at first to be an obstacle, can actually turn into selling points if you deal with them effectively.

If, however, you don't properly manage tension—at the first sign of the buyer's backup behavior—chances are the buyer's tension will begin to rise and his backup behavior will become more entrenched. The more frustrating the situation becomes for him, the less productive your sales call will be. When the buyer's tension has reached the "I can't take it anymore" level, you will begin to notice his backup behavior taking the place of his usual social style behaviors.

Under normal conditions, when you first meet buyers they are not exhibiting tension behavior. When they do become tense, however, you can be reasonably sure that they will show backup behavior. Your being able to pinpoint a client's backup behavior is very important in maintaining a good sales relationship. For instance, by your knowing how to use the LSCPA strategy that we'll discuss later in this chapter, you will manage to get a reticent or aggressive client back to friendly. You'll not only be able to get the situation back to a productive level, but you also will start solving the customer's problems.

Backup behavior is easy to recognize. How will you know when the Analytical has had enough of your generalizations or the Expressive enough of your data printouts? Because, depending on whether they are Ask- or Tell-Assertive, their behavior will take the form of either *fight* or *flight.* (See Exhibit 1.)

- Fight means that the Tell-Assertive buyer will confront the tense situation by either attacking or becoming autocratic. "I don't like the idea. A new computer system won't help our bottom line. It simply can't work at this company right now."
- Flight means that the Ask-Assertive buyer will retreat from the stressful situation by either acquiescing or avoiding. "I'm not sure if we're really interested in a new telephone system in the near future, but, sure, I'll listen to what you have to say. We might need new phones someday."

Backup behavior is completely natural. There is nothing wrong with it; it helps people deal with uncomfortable situations. The problem for you is that once the buyer starts showing this behavior, it is up to you to use your versatility to bring things back to a less stressful, productive level.

One very important thing to remember is that you have a

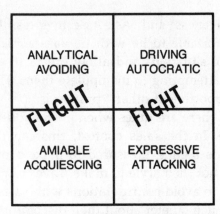

**Exhibit 1 Backup Behavior of the
Four Social Styles**

social style, too. It is very likely that if the customer is tense, you will show some tension too. Try to avoid this negativity. If you find yourself going into your own backup behavior in an already stressful situation, you will only add more tension and possibly ruin the relationship.

When two people with opposite social styles are in backup behavior, special problems can occur. An Ask-Assertive salesperson might become flustered and intimidated when a Tell-Assertive customer begins to attack. A Tell-Assertive salesperson might become restless and annoyed when an Ask-Assertive customer becomes quiet and doesn't communicate.

If both people are Tell-Assertive, there might be an out-and-out confrontation that leads nowhere except to slammed doors. If both are Ask-Assertive, both will have retreated into shells so that there will just be no more to say. Therefore, a big part of managing this kind of unproductive stress has to do with keeping your backup behavior in check.

AMIABLES AND TENSION

Amiables seem to be naturally friendly and versatile. They're able to reduce tension in most sales situations because of their

Emote-Responsiveness and Ask-Assertiveness. Many people find them comfortable to be with because Amiables don't attempt to control situations and allow others to express themselves without attempting to manipulate them. They listen and can be very supportive of others' proposals.

Of course, there are times when even good-natured Amiables are tense. In the sales context, this can happen if the Amiable buyer is feeling pressured to make a purchase decision. Since it is not their style to make waves or risk a relationship, they tend to avoid confrontations with salespeople.

They are much quieter about their discomfort than Expressives in that Amiables can simply ignore the salesperson's need for a firm commitment and not say anything definite. Of course, underneath it all the Amiable may be seething with resentment. To a Driver salesperson this could be exasperating—but it won't matter. If they are pressured further, they will mentally turn off your presentation and nothing will happen anyway.

Along these lines, Amiables appear to expect others in the sales situation to be "mind readers," to understand that they are unhappy. Then it is up to the other person, the offending party from the Amiable's view, to set things right. Naturally, it's not always possible to know exactly what's bothering the Amiable. You will have to work at getting him to divulge it. Meanwhile, if the tension level isn't brought down, the Amiable will either try to accommodate or acquiesce to keep the peace.

This means that Amiables either give up or give in. He or she may say in one way or another, "I give up. We'll do it your way! (Until I get the chance to do it my way!)" It's the part that he doesn't say that will hurt the relationship. You may think that everything's OK, until you try to close.

In the sales situation, you may find out too late that a decision not to buy from you was reached before you came through the door. For instance, John, an Amiable buyer, did not cancel the appointment with Sandy, the office supply sales rep, even though he had found a new supplier already who he and his staff was quite pleased with.

John may listen and respond to the sales rep politely or even positively. The Amiable may allow her to go so far as to write up an order. He may think that Sandy is a nice person and he doesn't want to hurt her feelings. Even though he does not want to order more office supplies, by placing an order, he will try to cut her presentation short to get her to leave. He does this so that he can avoid any more of the tension that he feels in this sales situation. Of course, the next day, he'll call to cancel the order.

ANALYTICALS AND TENSION

The Control-Responsive and Ask-Assertive behavior of the Analytical buyer can, in itself, cause tension for some salespersons, especially those who are Emote-Responsive. You may feel relationship tension because you perceive him as being emotionally reserved, not giving much in response to your presentation. His movements can be very controlled, he may smile very little if at all, even when he discusses his own ideas, he may not be very animated.

His deliberate, methodical approach to the sales situation can cause relationship tension. You may want to go on with your presentation, while he constantly interrupts you to ask for more details to back up your statements. A Driver salesperson may be tempted to glance at his watch with impatience. An Expressive may not want to deal with such "picky" facts at all.

You may also feel tense because this buyer's high dedication to the job at hand can be very demanding. If he is interested, he will want to thoroughly look at all aspects of your proposal before signing the purchase order. If you are not able to adequately respond the the Analytical's needs, he will become very tense.

When the situation has become too tense for the Analytical, his backup behavior—avoidance—will take over. He will walk away from the situation so that he is not exposed to the stress anymore. An example follows.

Julia, an Expressive, sells insurance to businesses. When she visits Maura, an educational book distributor, she notices that Maura's business-operations calculator is open and ready on her desk. After introductions, Maura indicates that she's ready to take a look at Julia's proposal. Julia is very pleased that her sales staff has prepared printouts with the appropriate estimates for Maura's business.

Maura asks Julia to explain the numbers. Julia gives the numbers just a surface treatment and goes on to show Maura a few of her company's brochures that extol the benefits of all of their insurance plans. Maura doesn't respond. When Julia is finished, Maura asks her again to explain the difference in cost in the two plans that have been printed out for her business. Julia thinks that she has already explained the differences in the plans. She quickly repeats what she just pointed out in the brochures about the general differences. Julia doesn't understand what happened when Maura ends the discussion with the statement, "I'd like more time to look this over. Thank you for coming in today."

The Analytical will express his unhappiness with the situation in terms of your proposed solution to his task needs. He probably has a specific idea of what he wants, and that is precisely what he wants you to provide.

He probably will not express anything negative about your personal relationship with him—since he is not especially interested in the personal aspects of the sales relationship anyway. In order to avoid an issue, he may focus attention on the minutest details of your proposal. If he becomes defensive when you ask for a direct response to what you have presented, you can certainly tell that he is using his avoidance backup behavior.

In the sales context, you may notice avoidance backup behavior in the way that this buyer refuses to see you, or cuts short your presentation, or doesn't answer questions, or just stays quiet. He may also refuse to study your recommendations or, finally, to make any buying decision at all. You may get the feeling that your carefully prepared proposal is stuffed in his file somewhere, and that when he hears your name, he automatically pushes a some-later-time button in his response. You will hear his avoidance if he says, "I don't want to talk about it now."

This flight behavior of Amiables and Analyticals will have to be dealt with if your sales relationship is going to develop productively. If the Amiable goes on acquiescing and the Analytical avoiding, you will obviously not be communicating with your buyer. The sales process will be stifled with both the salesperson and the buyer feeling extreme tension. So it is to your advantage to try to work out the problem before continuing with your sales presentation. Here's an example of how a Tell-Assertive salesperson was able to cope with this sort of backup behavior (Exhibit 2).

> David Barrie, a 31-year-old Expressive, has sold a new word processing system to a large and prestigious publishing company. He worked out the initial needs for a system upgrade with Amiable Jennifer Logan, the fortyish office manager. David is in the process of installing the system when he goes to Jennifer's executive office to meet with her about the maintenance and service agreement.
>
> David, rather aggressively steps into her office. "Morning, Jennifer. Well, the big day, eh?"
>
> Jennifer avoids looking at him. "Oh, morning."
>
> David is excited about the day's events. "We're unloading the crates on the dock right now. The first phase should be in place by three o'clock this afternoon. Phase two tomorrow."
>
> Jennifer still hasn't looked at him. "That's nice."
>
> "And that leaves the rest of the week for training your people, for some hands-on practice, and for debugging the software."
>
> Jennifer says sarcastically, "Oh, really?"
>
> David hasn't really noticed Jennifer's unusual behavior. "That 415 has been getting rave reviews. It's really going to make a difference in overall level of productivity. Your people will love it. It's pretty exciting, eh?"
>
> "Yes." Jennifer is very low key.
>
> David is starting to recognize that Jennifer may have a problem. He slows down a bit. "Well, I've brought all the documentation for the system. I think we ought to talk about a maintenance agreement since installation is already underway."

"Well, you seem to have all the bases covered, David."

"Here's a sample copy of the Operator's Manual." He places it on her desk.

"Hmmm."

"Now the service contract. I should talk that over with you because I want to make absolutely certain that you understand all the details."

Jennifer says, in a rather noncommittal tone, "Sure."

Let's stop this case here. Jennifer seems absolutely unwilling to talk. What would you do if you were David?

FLIGHT STRATEGY

When you notice that Ask-Assertive buyers have gone into backup behavior, your first action should be to draw them out. Of course, it isn't quite that easy because, to do this, you have to try getting them to open up enough to divulge what's bothering them.

Here are some ways of drawing out Amiables and Analyticals in backup behavior.

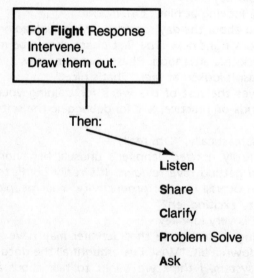

For **Flight** Response
Intervene,
Draw them out.

Then:

Listen

Share

Clarify

Problem Solve

Ask

Exhibit 2   Managing Flight Backup Behavior

- *Ask questions.*
  "Is there anything that I can help you with that I haven't covered?"
- *Be persistent in asking without being pushy.*
  "If you don't mind, I'd like to ask you what bothers you about this proposal?"
- *Try for specifics rather than vague answers.*
  "At this time, are there any features in this system that you really don't need? Would cutting them out help you keep within budget?"
- *Show genuine concern.*
  "There seems to be a problem. I really do want to hear what you have to say about this."
- *Acknowledge and confirm their feelings.*
  "Yes, I can understand why you might be hesitant about buying now."
- *Give them all the time they need to respond.*
  "Let's take as much time as we need to settle this. I do care about your concerns."
- *Mention your own feelings in the situation.*
  "I'm very sorry that this happened. I want to do whatever I can solve this problem."

Why is it important to draw out Ask-Assertive buyers? By doing this first, you can get their concerns out in the open so that you can deal with their problems. Also, by acknowledging their feelings, you reassure them that it is all right to disagree with you. This can be especially important if you are a Tell-Assertive salesperson dealing with an Ask-Assertive who is intimidated by what he perceives as your aggressive social style. It may encourage them to be more open in telling you their concerns the next time.

If you are not able to intervene in this manner and identify the cause of the buyer's discomfort, you may have difficulty solving the problem, and could risk the relationship and the sale. At the very least, the unproductive tension will increase on both sides. If the buyer really wants your product or service, the sales relationship will continue. What could be an important obstacle to the development of your sales relationship, however, may never be resolved.

LSCPA: A STRATEGY

After you have drawn out the buyer, you are ready to start the five-step strategy called LSCPA. Using LSCPA is very effective in dealing with both flight and fight backup behaviors.

Step L

Listen to the concern completely. Listen for the facts, the beliefs, and the feelings that are expressed.

If you are Tell-Assertive, don't show impatience; if you are Ask-Assertive, don't become intimidated by the buyer's negative remarks.

Step S

Share your appreciation of what the buyer is feeling or thinking. Allow the buyer to feel that you have his best interests at heart.

- Show empathy to the buyer.
- Respond to the facts and beliefs surrounding the concern.
- Respond to any feeling statement that the buyer makes.

Step C

Clarify the concern. You will not be able to solve the problem if you don't understand what it is.

- Restate the concern you hear to encourage the buyer to help you fully understand them.
- Ask questions to further clarify the concern.

Step P

Problem Solve when you understand the concern. Now that the problem is out in the open, it's time to do something to correct it. Even if you cannot solve the problem at the moment, show that you are willing to do something about it.

- Seek resolution of the buyer's concern.
- Work on a solution only after the concern has been thoroughly clarified and you are confident the buyer feels understood.
- State how you will solve the problem or dispel the buyer's concern.
- Make sure the solution addresses needs of the buyer's social style.

Step A

Ask if the concern had been satisfactorily addressed. If there are any further problems to resolve, they should be brought up here. If not, you can assume that for now things are settled.

- Agree on the solution.
- Make plans to follow through on the solution.

In an actual sales situation, you will not necessarily follow these steps in sequence, but rather use the steps that are appropriate throughout your discussion with a buyer. You may even have to go cycle back through these steps, especially "Clarify" and "Share," several times before you are able to ease the tension and understand the situation fully.

Let's go back to David and Jennifer. Notice how David uses some of these tension-reducing strategies. We'll pick up the conversation midway with David.

"Well, I've brought all the documentation for the system. I think we ought to talk about a maintenance agreement since installation is already underway."

"Well, you seem to have all the bases covered, David."

"Here's a sample copy of the Operator's Manual."

"Hmmm."

"Now the service contract. I should talk that over with you because I want to make absolutely certain that you understand all the details."

"Sure."

By this time, David realizes that Jennifer in backup. He begins trying to draw her out. "Jennifer, do you mind if I ask you something?"

"I suppose not."

"Well, you seem preoccupied this morning. That's not like you at all. Is there anything wrong?"

"No, not really." Jennifer is still not communicating.

"I mean, anything at all, really. Your concerns, large or small, are important to me. We've worked hard on this project, and I think we've built a relationship where we can level with each other."

"Well, frankly, David I'm a little disappointed in you."

"Oh. For what reason?"

"And a little hurt."

"Is it something that I've done or not done? I mean what seems to be the problem?"

"Bryce McCoy. That's the problem."

"Bryce McCoy? I don't understand."

"All this new equipment—the 415, as well as that new system we were thinking about . . ."

David wants to listen. "Yes?"

"You were dealing with me, David. I felt you knew that I'm the one entitled to the buying decision. This whole project to upgrade our capability is my responsibility."

"I realize that. Yes." David is sharing.

"So, then why did you go over my head?"

David needs clarification. "When?"

"With Bryce McCoy. Last week. Why did you and your manager use Bryce to speed up the timetable? I mean that makes me look bad. I trusted you, David. Why did you pull a stunt like that?"

David wants to share. "I need to hear this Jennifer. Can you tell me more about it?"

"That purchase order had my handwriting on it, but Bryce signed it, if you know what I mean. I mean my department does all of the work, and then you go to Bryce for sign off. How do you think that that reflects on us? How do you think that that makes me feel?"

"I see. Please, go on."

"I was ready to buy. You knew that. Didn't we have an agreement?"

"Yes."

"OK. So what's the deal? Why did you feel you had to go over my head?"

David offers information. "International Power Pac. We learned they were planning a competitive strategy. Bryce McCoy was their internal contact."

"Power Pac? They never came through the door."

"But we got word that they were going to."

"Oh, David."

It is time, again, for David to share. "Look, Jennifer, I'm sorry. I know how you must feel. I guess we overreacted. When we learned that Power Pac was going to make a desperate eleventh-hour bid, my district manager insisted on calling Bryce McCoy, and before we knew it we were in his office."

"Why didn't you phone me?"

David continues sharing. "I should have. I realize that now. But, Jennifer, I didn't mean to jeopardize our relationship by going to McCoy. In fact, I spoke to him about how valuable that relationship was. You should have been included, absolutely."

"Hmmm."

David begins to problem-solve. "And I'm wondering if you, me, Bill Curtis, and Bryce McCoy shouldn't sit down and go over what happened."

"What for?"

"Well, I could explain to him the work we did on that project, where we were going with it, and why we moved the way we did when we heard about Power Pac. I'd like to be able to demonstrate our good faith here. I know how the buying process works and which decisions you're entitled to Jennifer. And maybe McCoy should hear that from me."

"You know, David, it takes a long time to build the kind of trust that you and I have enjoyed in our business relationship. Don't you feel that you were a little shortsighted in making such an unprofessional move?"

"Yes, and it's important to me to regain that trust. What will it take? What can we do to 'right' this situation?"

"Well, first, I think I'd like your absolute assurance that such a thing won't happen again."

"I understand. And you have it."

"And as for a meeting with McCoy, well . . . I guess I'll have to give that further thought."

"Fine. You think it over." He indirectly asks her to consider it. "Now, let's take a look at this service contract. There are some complicated parts I want to make sure you . . ." And with the air cleared, the business of setting up the system can continue.

A quick analysis of David's strategy might go like this. David asked Jennifer if she had something on her mind. He drew her out by indicating that he needed to hear what she had to say even if he might not like it. Then he used LSCPA to correct his misunderstanding of her needs. The immediate problem of Jennifer's seeming lack of interest was resolved by David's idea to hold a meeting. Do you have any other ideas on what David could have done?

As an Expressive, David was careful not to become impatient with this flight behavior. Sometimes Tell-Assertives are tempted to skip the first three steps of Listening, Sharing and Clarifying and go right to Problem-solving. Taking this action might not allow a reticent Ask-Assertive buyer to fully explain the problem. He might also think that you're not really interested in his concerns.

We will take a look at the other side of backup behavior in the next chapter—that is, the fight behavior of the Tell-Assertives.

8

Tell-Assertive Backup Behavior: Fight

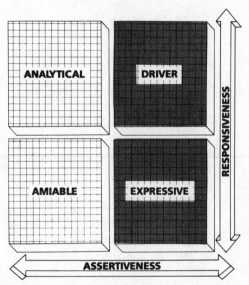

"Misunderstanding! Don't give me that. I'm up to here with new product roll-out, and you come in here with hidden costs. I took a big chance with you, Harry. I cut away from two old vendors because you convinced me M.J.P. could meet our specs and deliver at a competitive price. I think you're trying to squeeze me!"

While Ask-Assertives clam up, Tell-Assertives are very demonstrative in their backup behavior. Very different behavior, but both can have a disastrous effect on the sales process. Even though the styles are different, they are both telling you that something has gone wrong or that the buyer has a problem that you have not dealt with. If you are able to manage the tension in the relationship, you can bring the normal level of tension to the productive zone.

The LSCPA—Listen, Share, Clarify, Problem-solve, Ask—strategy that we discussed in Chapter 7 can be employed with the Tell-Assertives just as with the Ask-Assertives. So the LSCPA strategy should be your basic plan in dealing with backup behavior. As you probably realize, the drawing out process that you would use with Ask-Assertives is completely unnecessary with Drivers and Expressives who are attacking you or lecturing you about some problem. With them, you will want to let them vent, let them get their tension and problems out in the open before you try LSCPA. They will readily do this with little or no encouragement.

The two Tell-Assertive social styles both exhibit fight behavior in backup. However, Expressives attack, while Drivers become autocratic. So before coming up with an exact strategy for each one, let's take a deeper look at how each style responds to tension. (Refer to Exhibit 1 on p. 105.)

DRIVERS AND TENSION

Drivers can become very disappointed if the results of projects aren't as good as they expected. The Driver had this in mind when he agreed to do business with you. If your service or product doesn't perform as expected, you'll hear about it. The Driver's need for results should not be taken lightly. He expects the product or service to work as promised. He also expects you to be professional in your dealings with him. In the sales situation this can create tension in salespeople because of the Driver's great concern for getting the job done.

Carl, a Driver, is the manager of an accounting firm that specializes in handling tax matters for well-to-do business executives. They work very hard. Carl works very hard, until all hours of the night—especially around March and April.

He enjoys the satisfaction of his work but realizes that he would be more productive if he had a particular computer system. With this new system installed in January, Carl would be able to expand his business for the coming tax period. His staff would be trained and the bugs worked out.

In September he calls Norman, an Analytical sales rep for a computer company, to begin looking at machine capabilities and to discuss ideas for the system's configuration. That meeting goes well. Carl is impressed with Norman's knowledge and businesslike manner.

The next week Carl calls Norman to set up a meeting with him and his sales manager to finalize the deal. Carl is adamant about his need for these computers at a particular time. The sales manager assures Carl that this is the right system for his needs and that the time issue is no problem. Carl signs the purchase contract.

Delivery is set for the first week in January. Two weeks after the delivery date, when the system has not yet arrived, Carl cancels the order. He doesn't allow the sales manager to explain his situation. Carl controls the discussion by telling him of the general incompetence of his computer company.

For Carl, getting in the new system and training his employees would be too difficult to do before March. He will consider buying a system again next year. He thinks that by then there will be an even better system put on the market by another company.

The fact that Drivers like Carl depend on their ability to control situations by their Tell-Assertiveness means that they might not adequately communicate their own emotions. They'll tell you how their plans are not working out for their work projects, but they will not discuss how they personally feel about it. Instead of looking toward the personal side of the sales relationship, they use facts to move their aims forward. Under some circumstances, this task pressure can cause a considerable amount of tension for both the salesperson and the Driving buyer himself.

The Driver deals with this tension by going into an autocratic backup behavior. He will attempt to control the situation and the salesperson by using his power. He may attempt to belittle you and your company in the most logical way imaginable while remaining completely businesslike. Some might use reason, logic, and facts as weapons of control.

Another way that the Driver exhibits backup behavior has to do with the way he perceives his position. Status based on his or her accomplishments is very important to the Driver. In the sales situation, you might find the Driver using his or her job position—which, very likely, the Driver thinks is higher than yours—to get you to keep your distance. When the Driver is in backup, this distance is just what he wants. This can be a roadblock to your developing a friendly, personal relationship. You might be very discouraged by this rather cold attitude when you try to get through to Drivers to find out what the problems may be.

Rather than allow you to penetrate his emotional shield, the Driver can very abruptly cut you off. He may have to prepare for his staff meeting, interview a potential new employee, write a report, or whatever else in his action-packed schedule will get you to leave his office. Since this occurs after his logical explanation as to why he cannot work with you, he expects you to have understood his position. His typical end-of-discussion statement is "That's completely the wrong solution all around. The facts speak for themselves." No, don't try to argue with him. Use LSCPA.

EXPRESSIVES AND TENSION

Expressive buyers can also raise tension by way of their some- times blunt, direct statements. Because of their Emote-Respon- siveness they are, however, much more informal about it. They take disappointment personally and are much more willing than Drivers to let you know what they really feel.

So what you have to look out for in the sales situation are flying barbs. Be ready with a shield! The Expressive may let out with whatever words that will release his emotional tension in- cluding a personal attack against you. You'll have to be thick- skinned because the openness and directness of the Expressive can sometimes hurt.

Be assured that this surprisingly quick response to tension should be over soon—and that as judgmental as it all seemed, after this, the Expressive probably won't hold a grudge. The Expressive buyer's point will have been made, however, be- cause his emotional appeal can at times have more impact than an appeal to logic.

Carol owns several clothing retail stores in four relatively sophisticated college towns. Besides sweatshirts and jeans, a good portion of her business depends on what could be called "fad" clothes. In order to keep her competitive edge, she asks clothing wholesalers for exclusives on some of their lines in each town.

She's a good customer—Carol buys more from them than the other store owners—so they usually comply. They allow her to have first pick of their newest samples. Her customers know to come to her first when they want to be "the first on their block" with the latest rage. She thinks that this "with-it" reputation is what her business depends on.

Her relationship with Judy, a salesperson for a clothing

importer, has been good. Today, however, Carol is raving mad. She saw that Judy has sold to a nearby competitor a line of clothing that is very similar to the one she bought—and less expensive.

Judy lets Carol vent her anger. She hears about how her company and Judy herself have terrible taste in clothing. When she finishes, Judy tells her she's sorry that this has happened but that the lines that the other store chain bought were frankly cheap. Carol's stores are known for carrying quality clothing— and that's exactly what Judy sold her. Carol agrees and places an order for the next season's line.

Judy has known Carol for a long time. She understands Carol's tirades—that they should be listened to and dealt with immediately. She also knows that there is an element of trust in their relationship so that it is safe to allow Carol to argue, even though she may say some unpleasant things about her.

Although previously the Expressive may have verbally attacked you, your best advice is not to do the same with him. If you hurt his self-esteem, he'll find a means of getting out of the sales relationship. If he can't do that because he depends on your products, he may pick up where he left off in his attack on you, your company, and your products or services. This backup behavior has as its theme "This (meaning you, your company, ideas, etc.) is ridiculous. What are you trying to do, make us the laughing stock of the industry?" As with the Driver, it is pointless to fight back. Let him vent and use LSCPA.

Here's another look at how this strategy can work with Tell-Assertive buyers.

Mitchell Prescott, an Expressive buyer, is not very happy with the outcome of his purchase from Harry Woodridge, an Ask-Assertive salesperson. Mitchell is the Managing Director at a high-tech assembly operation for advanced electrical hearing products. Harry is sales rep for M.J.P., an electronics supply firm.

When Harry walks into Mitchell's office, Mitchell is angry, but trying to control himself. He waves an invoice at Harry.

"You know, Harry, based on what we talked about, I

projected a cost of $400 a unit. Your invoice here puts the cost at $403 a unit. What's going on here?"

"Oh, that would be the addition for up-front costs on research and design." Harry manages to maintain his composure even though he knows that Mitch is angry.

"Oh great! Just great. Boy, you've got a lot of nerve, you know that."

"Mitch, I'm sorry. Is there some misunderstanding?" Mitch doesn't really understand what the fuss is about.

"Misunderstanding! Don't give me that. I'm up to here with new product roll-out, and you come in here with hidden costs. I took a big chance with you, Harry. I cut away from two old vendors because you convinced me M.J.P. could meet our specs and deliver at a competitive price. I think you're trying to squeeze me!"

Let's stop Mitch in mid-attack. As an Expressive he certainly responds to tension much more aggressively than does Amiable Jennifer. Simply put, the Tell-Assertive comes on strong. Unlike Ask-Assertives, who you must work at drawing out, Tell-Assertive buyers will not hesitate in letting you know what the problem is right away—either by the autocratic stance of Drivers or the verbal attack of Expressives. How would you cope with Mitch's backup behavior?

As we've mentioned, with Tell-Assertives, the first thing a salesperson should do in responding to fight backup behavior is to let the buyer vent his or her feelings (Exhibit 1). Some effective ways of doing this are to

- *Get out of their way.* Beware of flying words, or objects.
- *Accept their comments without judgment or automatic rebuttal.* If you cannot resist the temptation—particularly if you are another Tell-Assertive person—to argue with this buyer, you will find yourself in a very negative, unproductive situation.
- *Encourage them to talk to get out their feelings and to get past the attack to identify the real problems that may be behind their anger.* Remember that after they release the initial tension, they will want to talk more reasonably about what's bothering them.

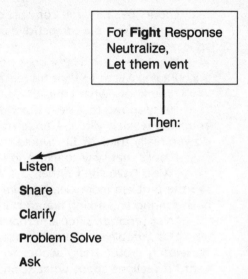

Exhibit 1   Managing Fight Backup Behavior

- *Attempt to diffuse their anger by allowing them to vent their feelings.* If you allow them to freely express their anger, you will have an easier time of having a quieter discussion later.

It is strategically important to try to neutralize the fight behavior by allowing the buyer to express their discomfort. By listening to their anger, you are showing that you accept their differences with you and that you are willing to work with them. This can translate to mean that you value their business.

As with the Ask-Assertives, once the problem is aired and addressed, it is easier to get back to the sales task. You may even have gained a few points, by showing the buyer that you can be trusted to be a an effective problem-solver in the future. And, again, if the tension is not managed and is allowed to increase, the sale may be lost.

Let's see how these strategies work with Mitch and Harry.

"Misunderstanding! Don't give me that. I'm up to here with new product roll-out, and you come in here with hidden costs. I took a big chance with you, Harry. I cut away from two old vendors because you convinced me M.J.P. could meet our specs and deliver at a competitive price. I think you're trying to squeeze me!"

"Squeeze you?" Harry does not say this defensively. He is encouraging Mitch to vent his feelings.

"You know what I mean!"

Harry shows that he is sharing Mitch's feelings. "Yes, I do, and believe me, Mitch, I understand why you're upset, but do you really think M.J.P. would try to squeeze you?"

"Looks that way to me. And I don't like it."

"Well, I wouldn't either, if I were you. Mitch, I'd like to see the problem more clearly, from your perspective." Harry is both sharing and asking him to clarify his concern.

"Not problem, singular. Problems, plural, with an 's.'"

"OK, problems. I'm still concerned about this business of 'squeezing' you." Harry wants to give Mitch more room to vent his feelings about what seems to him to be considerable concerns.

"Everything seems to happen at once. One big happy co-incidence. A design problem here, a manufacturing delay there, pressure from marketing . . . and then you come through the door with increased costs."

"So this new product roll-out hasn't been too smooth." Harry is sharing.

"Thirty-five miles of bumpy road."

Harry needs more clarification. "Are you on target?"

"Oh, yeah. End of July."

"Well, how does the market look?"

"Looks good. The forecast is good."

"But you've got some concerns."

"Yes. Marketing and Sales have been all over the industry raising expectations—high expectations. We're nervous. This is the most sophisticated product we've ever developed."

"You've had a lot on your mind."

"And your surprise billings aren't helping, either."

"So our communication was off, wasn't it?"

"It's more than just a matter of communciation. Now I hope you're not going to stand here and tell me that this addition isn't going to affect our bottom line."

"No. I wouldn't do that. What concerns me, however, is that I wasn't aware of this new line of yours, and so I wasn't able to give you the kind of cost formulas and support you needed."

"Well, that's been under wraps. There was no reason for you to know."

Now that the problem has been adequately clarified, Harry wants to start problem-solving. "I see. But maybe we could have worked something out that would have been more understandable. Maybe we can still work something out."

"Like what?"

"Well, several options. We can bill you separately for R and D which allows you to keep your cost per unit in line as projected, and we'll carry that cost until your product takes off. Then you can offset the cost of R and D with a volume discount."

"Hmmm."

Harry picks up the invoice from Mitch's desk. "I'll get our billing department to issue another invoice—let them know what's going on. You know, Mitch, as a supplier, M.J.P. is vitally interested in the whole chain, right to the end user. We want to be responsive."

"OK, sounds good. Let's get to it."

In working with Mitch, Analytical Harry did not get stuck in the biggest trap Ask-Assertives could get into with angry Tell-Assertives. He did not allow himself to become intimidated. He was also willing to take the risk of listening and asking for more information about Mitch's concerns. In this case, LSCPA worked to everyone's advantage.

Now that you know about normal and backup behavior for the four social styles, in Chapter 9 we will begin looking at what this all means in the total sales situation. That is, we will develop strategies for dealing with Amiables and Analyticals.

9

Strategies for Selling to Ask-Assertive Buyers

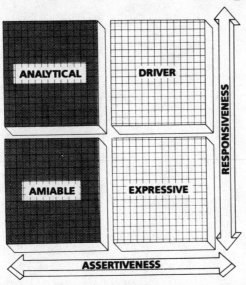

Customers of both styles tend to listen more than talk, follow rather than lead, and generally act in a low-key manner.

By now you've seen examples of versatility. You know that being a versatile salesperson means being able to adapt to the needs and characteristics of customers of the four basic social styles. Showing that you understand and can work with your clients' personal needs and their expectations in the sales relationship will help keep your relationships with them in the productive tension zone.

In the sales situation, you will know how to maintain a good balance in the task and relationship areas. You will be able to cope with any of your clients' backup behaviors that may surface from time to time. You'll also be able to control yourself whenever you feel that your side of the situation is becoming too tense.

Just as you will want to deal with each customer individually according to his or her social style, you will also want to develop a separate selling strategy for each style. In this chapter we will describe plans for dealing with Ask-Assertives—Amiables and Analyticals.

SELLING TO AMIABLE BUYERS

As we have seen, Amiables are usually cooperative and friendly in their relationships with salespeople. They are very relationship oriented. As long as the salesperson understands this buyer's need for personal assurances and sensitivity to his or her feelings—from the salesperson as well as from the buyer's own staff—relationship tension should be kept to a minimum.

An Amiable, however, can be put off if, in his view, a salesperson seems too task oriented and aggressive in selling instead of relating personally to the people involved with the purchase. So for dealing with the Amiable customer you should come up with an approach that respects his casual, open, deliberate, and friendly way of doing business.

Getting an Appointment

Amiables like to receive introduction letters with a personal, friendly touch. Your first step should be to send one to this potential buyer. Keep in mind, though, that being friendly does not mean that the letter should be very personal and completely unbusinesslike.

For starters, he would appreciate knowing who you are and why you're contacting him. It would help for you to emphasize

- *Your experience working with clients who the Amiable knows.* These other clients can be known by the Amiable either by reputation (he has heard of the client) or by experience (he personally knows the client).
- *Your reliability and follow-through.* Let him know why he should trust and depend on you and your company.
- *The quality of your product or service.* He also wants to be able to depend on your product. He wants to be sure that it is the right one to help him solve his business problems.

Set aside a comfortable time to follow this introductory letter with a friendly personal phone call. It is with this call that you can begin to establish trust in the sales relationship with the Amiable. Allow yourself to be friendly, open, honest, and sincere. With this approach to the initial phone call, you'll have a much easier time beginning work with the Amiable when you actually meet with him. This phone call can have another use. It can give you conversation ideas for starting your sales call.

Opening the Call

At the beginning of your first and all sales meetings with the Amiable, you should engage in pleasant, casual conversation. With this client, it would be a mistake to start by immediately discussing business.

What should come through on your part in this conversation is that you're really interested in the Amiable's work and personal goals. You should be sincere about this. Your learning more about these aspects of the Amiable's life will help you to earn the right to work productively with this customer in the sales relationship.

Simply giving details of your product or service knowledge, may not be convincing enough with the Amiable. Try coming up with someone who you have worked with who the Amiable knows and, you would hope, trusts. Use this common acquaintance as a reference. The Amiable will feel better about dealing with you if he knows that he can ask someone else about you and your product or service.

Discovering Buyer Needs

Amiables, more than the other social styles, need to feel that they are working in a cooperative, friendly atmosphere. With this kind of positive work environment, they feel free to discuss their feelings with you and to exchange information that is pertinent to the sale. They will open up with questions and ideas that will help you to help them. A trusting sales relationship can be further developed if the two of you maintain this balance.

You may find yourself listening very carefully to Amiables in order to get to the real point of what their goals are. Sometimes the Amiable customer may seem to be rather shy about stating exactly what he or she needs. This client will tend to hint at his goals by using understatements.

One way to get beyond this indirect communication is simply to question the Amiable. Try keeping to specifics. In other words, you may find yourself questioning on exact points so that the Amiable will answer in more specific terms than he is used to doing.

Remember that the Amiable, just like your other customers, does have long-range goals and does want to accomplish them. It is just that he may be a little quieter about expressing them. He will be very pleased with you if you help him to state these goals and then follow up by assisting him in achieving the accomplishments that he hopes for.

Since the Amiable responds to, relatively speaking, a more subdued approach, you would do best if you keep your questions low-key. Try not to hit the Amiable with rapid-fire questions. This would be too aggressive for him.

When the Amiable answers, listen responsively. Be patient. This will be very much appreciated. The Amiable likes to be encouraged to express himself. If you give plenty of both verbal and nonverbal feedback, the Amiable customer will feel free to open up. Your encouraging responses will give him the emotional space to communicate.

Of course, you are meeting with the Amiable customer on business—no matter how friendly the conversation may seem. You may have to extract his company's information about any unresolved budget issues. Cost justification points may not come so easily from him either. So it's up to you to ask. It is likely that he'll understand why you need to know this information and will cooperate in giving it to you.

At times, a sales call with an Amiable customer may ramble a bit. In this case, one or both of you may find that you're losing track of the important points that are being covered in this meeting. You both can find it helpful if, from time to time during the visit, you summarize what you believe you've heard to be the Amiable's key ideas and feelings. Focusing in on these main points can give a clearer perspective on what the customer needs and how you can help him.

Making a Recommendation

Your summaries during the visit will make it easier for you to make a recommendation. At this point, you'll want things to be clearly defined. Put your ideas in writing and go over them with the customer.

What is important is that you are sure the Amiable understands what you are saying that you can and will do. These statements should be in support of the Amiable's personal goals. Of course, this will be in the context of his business. The Amiable, however, will be more responsive if tasks are presented in ways that reflect the positive aspects of your personal relationship with him.

The Amiable will also want to have in writing the specifics on what you will contribute and what he needs to contribute. Again, cooperation is the key here. Encourage it on his part and, as for you, show that you will do whatever you have to so that he can succeed in reaching his goal.

Your written recommendation should also include information on what you and your company will do to support the project. Explain the resources that you are willing to commit in support of his purchase of your product or service.

What you are doing is providing a basis for the Amiable to consider buying from you. The Amiable customer needs to know—as clearly as possible—that he can trust you and your company. This recommendation should assure him that your solution is the best solution to his needs. You want him to believe that if he follows your ideas that there will be no need for him to consider others.

If the Amiable customer is not the final decision maker,

encourage him to invite this person to meet with both of you. The Amiable is comfortable with staff cooperation and will feel more confident in working with you if the purchase decision maker is in on the sales process.

Even with this involvement of the decision maker, the Amiable himself may seem to be in constant need of assurance. You can satisfy this need by making sure that he understands that your solution is not only the best for the present situation but that it will also serve him well in the future.

If necessary, show him how well your product or service has worked over time with a common acquaintance. This kind of third party personal recommendation of you and your company can have a very positive effect on the ultimate sale. The Amiable will respond better to personal testimonials than he will be brochures and printouts that explain in technical detail why your product or service is the best for him.

Asking for the Business

Most important in dealing with the Amiable buyer is that you remember not to push him to buy. If you don't realize that you're doing this, you will know when you begin to notice that the Amiable is going into backup behavior. If he begins to acquiesce to what he feels are your demands, then you will understand that you have to soften your approach.

Asking for the order indirectly tends to work best with the Amiable customer. His relationship orientation will be dominant here. Unlike the Driver who may just want to sign the purchase order and be done with it, the Amiable will want more time to work up to the signing. For him, this will help him to feel that the purchase is a natural outcome of your relationship.

You can help things progress, if you emphasize what you are guaranteeing the customer. That is, show him how you are doing the best you can to protect him from any potential mishap in this sale.

In keeping with this, allow the Amiable to know what his alternatives are if something unexpected does go wrong. He doesn't want to feel cornered in the sales relationship. The Amiable must be allowed to feel that there is a way out for him if it becomes necessary.

Giving him such a contingency plan can help you to make the sale. This may not seem like the most positive approach. You would hope that his decision to buy is based on your original recommendation. It will, however, provide a guard against his winding up with "buyer's remorse" if things do not work out as planned.

Follow up is very important to the Amiable. In particular, he wants to be assured that you will be personally involved in the process after he decides to buy. Since he has spent so much time and energy in building a sales relationship with you he will want to know that you will be available during the follow up. Tell him that you will be there.

If there are still some questions to be answered, encourage the Amiable to bring in other staff members to your discussions. Involving others in the final buying decision can help him to feel that his inclination to buy from you would, in fact, benefit others. It will help him to trust his own decision-making ability and will give him the confidence he needs to say yes to your proposal.

Do not be put off by the Amiable's objections. Actually, welcome them. Your being patient and thorough in answering them can really pay off for you. You can reassure this customer by being as open and honest as possible. You should be positive in expressing exactly how they will be affected by their decision to buy your product or service.

If you find that you cannot adequately answer a question, bring in an expert. Expert assurance is especially liked by Amiables. The expert can either be someone who is particularly knowledgeable in your field or it can be someone who the Amiable respects who is familiar with your company and what it has to offer.

Although some details may be bothersome to Amiables, another means of assuring this customer is by justifying the purchase in financial terms. You do not want to overwhelm him with facts and figures, however, it will certainly help to explain to him what exactly he is getting for his money. Show him how this purchase can pay for itself or even allow him to save in other areas in the future.

How the Amiable client personally feels about making the purchase will be the most important factor for you to consider. The more comfortable he is, the easier it will be for both of you to progress in the sales relationship. If you are not sure of how he feels, ask him. Deal with his conflicts and objections as they occur.

Installing and Implementing the Solution

The Amiable would likely be very upset if, after he signs the purchase order, you disappear. He expects his relationship with you to continue. You will live up to his expectations if you make a follow-up appointment with him.

Your first order of business at this next meeting is to congratulate the Amiable on his decision to buy. Showing that you care about what he did and that you feel positively about it will help him to feel better about it himself. It will help him to quiet any lingering doubts about what he has done. Also, by this time you should have a reasonably friendly relationship. Your sincere congratulations will let him know that you think highly of him.

Business necessities come next. He will want to know about your implementation plan. Who are and what is involved. What does he have to contribute. What is your part in the implementation.

He will also need to know how all this will occur. Giving him a well-planned schedule of events will be very helpful. This will allow him to prepare his staff so that things will flow as smoothly as possible.

It's important for both of you that the payment plan is exactly spelled out. Work with him on coming up with a mutually acceptable payment schedule. By taking time with these arrangements, you can avoid future conflicts.

After this meeting, maintain contact with the Amiable buyer. Schedule as many contacts as possible so that you can provide services that he may need. For example, you can monitor the progress of the installation by getting periodic reports. If the buyer hasn't mentioned it, these reports can indicate a need for more service from your company. Offering this help will be appreciated by the Amiable.

The need for training of the Amiable's staff, or more training than was originally expected, can become obvious to you if you take the time to visit the installation. The Amiable may be having huge headaches because of this but his agreeable nature may keep him from complaining to you. If you see the need for more training, offer a new training plan. Things will go much smoother for the Amiable and his staff.

Do you see a need for new or different services when you have your follow-up meetings? That is, are there any snags in the installation? Any problems with the original plan? Or, does the buyer have any new problems that can be helped by a revision in the installation? The buyer may not be aware that you can help him or, for whatever reason, he may not be able to ask you to help him. If you see any of this as a need, do not hesitate to recommend the introduction of new services from your company.

During all your follow-up visits, just as before, listen carefully to the Amiable buyer. Maintain the positive relationship even if some of the issues that he brings up seem to be very minor, or even trivial, to you. There are times, with the Amiable, that what may be expressed as something of little importance is actually a shield used for hiding a much larger concern. So, in order to keep the relationship in the productive tension zone, always remember to listen to him. And listen responsively.

SELLING TO ANALYTICAL BUYERS

Like the Amiable, the Analytical social style is Ask-Assertive. Customers of both styles tend to listen more than talk, follow rather than lead, and generally act in a low-key manner. It's about here where the similiarities end, however. Your approach to the Analytical buyer is a lot more businesslike than your dealings with the Amiable.

Getting an Appointment

As with the Amiable, your introduction to the Analytical buyer should be by way of a letter. Unlike the friendly letter that you would send to the Amiable, the letter to the Analytical should be completely businesslike.

In your discussion about your product or service, you should give specific, detailed information. Being vague about this will not serve to positively influence the Analytical to set up an appointment with you. He might actually dismiss you as not having enough substance to help him problem solve.

Just as you would be specific about your product or service, you would also give details about yourself. Let this buyer know who you are. What are your professional credentials? Give him good reason for accepting you in the sales relationship.

The same goes for information about your company. He will want to know your company's background. Highlight your company's noteworthy accomplishments. Remember that the Analytical is task oriented and wants to work with a company that shows a high regard for helping its clients reach their goals.

You can indicate this by referring to another customer who had success by using your product or service. As with the Amiable, the Analytical does appreciate the assurance of knowing that others have benefited from your company. There is a difference here, however. The Analytical is not particularly interested in personal testimonials. He is more interested in examples from others as to the specifics of how your product or service worked. The Analytical will want to apply this information to his own situation.

Overall, your letter should tell the Analytical how your product or service works. You can provide him with some information about how your product will be cost effective for him and his company. Don't be afraid to give him some numbers on this subject.

You should also emphasize your company's stability. As your company's representative, you should tell him of your experience with this product or service so that he'll be able to trust your knowledge and stability, too.

This rather detailed letter should serve as a good introduction. Your follow-up phone call should also be specific. In your call, you should explain how long you expect your first meeting to be with the buyer. The Analytical will also want to know what you expect to accomplish during this meeting. He wants to know your plans so that he can decide beforehand whether that is the way that he wants to spend his time.

Opening the Call

You have gotten past the first hurdle; you have scheduled an appointment for the first sales call. The best advice now is to come prepared. Don't underestimate the need to come well-armed with background information about you, your company, and your expertise. Bring brochures, sales kits, printouts, whatever at all you need to provide thorough background information. You can never have too much information with this buyer.

Just as the Analytical expects you to be an expert in what you do, treat him as if he were an expert in his area. In this respect, you are approaching him as if you were an advisor or a consultant. Unlike the Amiable, he does not expect or even necessarily want you to be a friend. He wants you to be businesslike and knowledgeable.

The best way to live up to his expectations is to do your homework. The Analytical looks for substance. He wants to be sure that you thoroughly understand his situation and needs. He may think that you are wasting his time if your knowledge of this isn't clearly evident.

How he uses time is very important to the Analytical. Many Analytical buyers can seem to be extremely structured in their use of time to salespersons of other styles. You should be conscious of this and respect his need for every minute to count in making progress toward his goals.

Discovering Buyer Needs

It's unlikely that the Analytical will want to engage in a lot of small talk. Save that for the Amiable. Instead, in this case, think of the meeting as a productive exchange of information.

It might help you if, in preparing for the sales call, you come up with a detailed outline of the information that you believe will help this buyer solve his problem. If you approach him with a well-organized, systematic approach to your material about your product or service, the Analytical will be more receptive to you.

As your presentation continues, you will be able to get a good idea of the client's needs because it's very likely that he will ask good questions based on how your product or service might help him. This, in turn, will help you to define his needs as it relates to what you have to offer him. Your preparation will make it easier to answer him. This should lead to a comprehensive exchange of information that will benefit both of you.

When you see this happening in a meeting with an Analytical, you can fairly judge that things are going positively so far. With a good base of factual information already covered, you can begin to encourage the Analytical to discuss his own ideas. Allow him to express his "expert" opinions on what you've presented.

If he seems to be willing to express his feelings, than certainly encourage that, too. It will help you to gain a better understanding of what this buyer needs. Allow the conversation to take as long as it has to. It's best not to indicate that you're in a hurry. The Analytical likes having the time to thoroughly deal with all the facts.

The Analytical can appear to dissect the facts to minutia from the point of view of the other social styles, particularly the Expressives. If you think that you are listening to more about the situation than you feel you will ever have to know, well, then check yourself. Be patient. The Analytical will not buy unless he is sure of all the facts. As the salesperson, it's up to you to provide them, and even help analyze them thoroughly if that's necessary.

The Analytical is looking for your support in their thinking. He wants to know that you are aligned with his ideas. Let him know that you are—and this, of course, means paying close attention to his thoughts. Show him that you are prepared to support his ideas with your product or service so that he can reach his objectives.

All of this becomes a comprehensive discovery process for the Analytical. The information that you bring to your presentation plays a big role in this process. Taking your time with this part of the sales relationship will pay off later with this buyer. When you need to justify your recommendations and handle objections, you will have the groundwork set.

Making a Recommendation

When you are ready to make a recommendation, take a written proposal to the Analytical in person. As with your previous dealings with this buyer, the recommendation must be detailed.

The strongest point that you make should be the cost justification for his purchase of your product or service. Back this up with all the numbers. This financial data should include information on how you arrived at the figures. If you do not include this information, you can certainly expect the Analytical to ask you for it. Don't come up short here. His trust will be hard to come by without a strong case for the cost of your proposal.

Having all the data is not enough. You should give it to him in a well-organized and systematic format. The facts in your presentation should be precise and to the point. No vague statements here, please, and no exaggerations either.

There's a good possibility that the Analytical will have questions for you. If you have difficulty with some of the specifics that the Analytical needs to know, avoid trying to make up an answer that sounds good to you or simply avoiding the question all together. Instead, tell him that you will research the answer in references or that you will ask an expert. Then remember to follow-through with the answer.

Throughout this sales relationship your approach should be reserved. Temper any of your own natural flamboyance—if you are so inclined—in order to work more effectively with the relatively subdued Analytical. He will appreciate a decisive, businesslike salesperson. However, he might not respond well to you if you appear too aggressive from his standpoint.

Emotional appeals do not usually go over well with Analyticals. He will not necessarily care that other companies have bought your product or service. So, it's best to limit using these points as evidence that the Analytical, too, should buy from you. At best, they can be used to give more specific examples as to how your product works.

Since the Analytical responds well to decisiveness, you'll do well to recommend a specific course of action. He does not need a series of alternatives to your original proposal for him to decide to buy. What he's looking for is a solid proposal that he can count on to provide exactly what he needs.

Give this buyer the chance to step ahead and take a look at all the purchase and delivery documents that you can provide. In other words, you are giving him everything that he needs to make a logical decision. He will see the full scope of his purchase from signing the purchase order to taking delivery.

At this stage, if the buyer needs some reasonable amount of time to think over your proposal, allow him to have it. He'd probably like to be able to review the details of your recommendations. He wants to be sure that they will help him accomplish his task needs.

Asking for the Business

Feel free to ask directly for the Analytical's order. Do not, however, become more aggressive at this point. Maintain your low-key approach.

It would not be unusual for an Analytical buyer to want to negotiate changes on the details in what you might consider to be standard paperwork. Be prepared for this by thinking through the Analytical's possible changes beforehand. Decide what your limits are and be ready with details to support your side of the negotiation. If you have good reasons, the buyer will understand your company's position.

What you're doing is working for a commitment now. As we've seen, the Analytical has a tendency to delay decisions. This can take the form of asking for more information so that he can make a knowledgeable decision later. You, the salesperson, can never be sure when "later" will happen. Your best defense is to have as much information as possible immediately available. This will help you avoid the Analytical's excuses for signing the purchase order now.

The information that you bring up should include your company's record. These facts can stand alone without the need for more analysis. Telling him of your company's service capabilities will indicate how you and your company can be depended upon to follow up on the sale.

Treat any of the Analytical's objections with objectivity. Respond to him by showing that you respect his buying needs and guidelines. Again, keep your ideas aligned with his.

Installing and Implementing the Solution

Your implementation plan must be specific. The Analytical buyer will want you to establish how the responsibilities are divided up at this stage. That is, what are your responsibilities and what are his. This should be exactly spelled out so that everyone involved has a clear understanding of what is expected.

A PERT chart or something similar can provide a very adequate plan for implementation. This will show how and when the various steps of the implementation procedure will take place. The Analytical buyer will appreciate this information.

For your follow-up, you should maintain periodic, regular contact with the Analytical buyer. Make sure that the implementation process is satisfactory from the buyer's viewpoint and that it is on schedule. If things are not going smoothly, you should be able to provide quick, thoughtful alternatives to get things rolling.

IN SUMMARY

With both Ask-Assertives—the Amiable and the Analytical—your approach to the sales relationship will be low-key. However, the Amiable expects a relatively friendly relationship while the Analytical wants a more businesslike attitude. The Amiable needs personal assurances and the Analytical wants detailed information. Although in neither case would an seemingly aggressive salesperson be appreciated, the strategies for dealing with each style is very different and specific.

In Chapter 10, we'll discuss strategies for dealing with the Tell-Assertives, the Drivers and the Expressives. With them, too, their differences make it necessary to come up with individual strategies for each style.

10

Strategies for Selling to Tell-Assertive Buyers

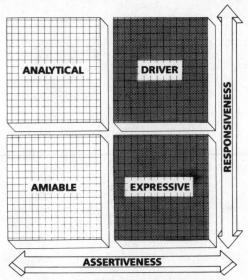

Just as with the Amiables and Analyticals, there are two distinct strategies for dealing with the Tell-Assertives—the Drivers and Expressives. Both of these Tell-Assertives tend to be fast paced and direct, but in your sales approach you should take their individual differences into account.

Maintaining a productive sales relationship with a Driver depends on how you're able to show him that you can help him achieve his task goals. In his business dealings, accomplishment—at times, his individual accomplishment—is what he strives for. If you can show him that you understand and can help him meet his objectives, you have a good chance at a positive relationship with him.

SELLING TO DRIVER BUYERS

Drivers in business usually are—or would like to be—very busy people. Because they are goal-oriented, they may ignore or overlook anything that doesn't seem to have to do very directly with what their individual plans or needs are. If you send an introductory letter to the Driver, he may avoid reading it. Although you may have clearly indicated how you are able to help him, he may see reading a letter as a waste of his time, especially if he doesn't know you or your company.

To introduce yourself, you may find it preferable to contact the Driver buyer first by phone. This introductory phone call should be businesslike and to the point. This is not the time to engage in friendly conversation. Let him know who you are and which of his business problems you can help him solve with your product or service. Then you would simply ask for an appointment. This is all the time you should spend on this first phone call.

A follow-up letter would be in order. In this letter you would confirm the time and date of the agreed upon appointment. However, you can also include whatever sales materials that you think the buyer would like to review before the meeting. This will help him to clarify some of the issues that he would like to bring up with you.

Opening the Call

The Driver will assume that you understand the specific business problem that you have offered to address. It's important for you to show him that this is indeed true. Establish that you are knowledgeable about his needs. Give him insights— related to your product or service—on how you can help him. You will notice that there is no time, or very little, spent here on friendly conversation. The Driver wants to get to the point from the start.

And sticking to the point as the meeting continues is equally important. During your discussion with the Driver he may appear to be completely focused on accomplishing a particular goal. He wants you to be just as focused on it as he is. Listen carefully to what he has to say. Give your complete attention to his ideas and objectives.

Throughout the meeting, the Driver will expect you to be businesslike. There should be a certain formality and reserve in your presentation. However, this does not mean that you should be cold in relating to him. By all means, be personable and cordial—just don't overdo the friendliness.

So that all the details of the buyer's business problem will be firmly established, go over all the factual information that has to do with it. With the details of the problem thoroughly understood, you can present likely results that he can expect when the customer uses your product or service. These expected results should be presented with factual evidence to justify them. The Driver is ever alert to what may seem to him to be vague claims.

Your presentation should occur as quickly as possible. You should keep to schedule—Drivers value punctuality. This buyer wants to think that his time is being spent efficiently. You have no room for rambling in your discussion. This may be a bit difficult for Expressive and Amiable salespersons, however, do try to stay on track.

Discovering Buyer Needs

The Driver likes to feel that he is in control of the situation. In his view, you are there to help him with his problem, not to present your own view on how he should be running his office or business. He expects you to know this and to defer to him whenever it's necessary.

Along these lines, he will not appreciate it if you take the initiative to tell him what you think he needs. A much more positive approach for him would be to ask him what he thinks his problems are. Ask him direct, fact-finding questions. What you want to know is what the Driver values. What the Driver finds rewarding may also be of interest. You'll find this useful to know when you make your recommendation.

One of the most annoying things to this client is to have his priorities in a fuzzy state. Work with him to clarify his priorities. Make sure that both of you know what they are. If you are not sure, ask.

When you ask questions, they should be consistent with your original reason for making the call. In other words, they should be obviously related to the issues at hand. Each answer will then fall in place to give you and the Driver buyer a better perspective on both your objectives.

The give-and-take of questioning will most likely lead to more questions on the Driver's part. If any questions come up that you are unable to answer, follow up the sales call by sending him or calling him with any information that he may have requested—immediately. He will appreciate your consideration and businesslike approach.

In this part of the process, your approach will be to support the Driver's beliefs, conclusions, and actions. You will want him to understand how you can positively help him to achieve his goals by taking care of his business needs. Having a clear-sighted view of his expectations will help you considerably when you get to the recommendation stage.

Making a Recommendation

The Driver customer is one who likes to make up his own mind. He might be put off if you simply offer him one solution to his problem. He may feel that you have attempted to make his decision for him.

Keeping this in mind, you can present your recommendation with alternatives. That is, you can give him alternate solutions to his needs by using your product or service. You would include with these alternatives, the outcomes that each will probably produce.

With all of the options that you offer him include documentation. He wants to know the facts on each. This is how he can come up with an intelligent choice. Yes, it may seem like this is a lot more work for you—some work that's completely unnecessary because all except one alternative will very likely be discarded. The courtesy of providing this information will not be lost with this customer. He will appreciate it. And, for you, it will help keep the sales relationship in the productive tension zone.

The Driver does like to have documentation that is as specific and factual as possible. However, unlike the Analytical, the Driver will feel overwhelmed if you give him too many details. This customer, remember, is interested in the big picture. He'll want to have details that adequately fill in the outline. If he's given more than that, you may find that he becomes very impatient.

One thing to remember in presenting alternatives to the Driver: Offer him the best quality possible. Of course, he has cost limitations, but within those boundaries find the best for him that you can. The Driver does not want to skimp on things that can have an impact on his goals.

When you get to the summary section of the recommendation, consider giving a quick overview of what you've covered. It would be best not to single out a specific plan of action that you think would be best for the customer. Allow the Driver to make the choice.

Most of all, what you are doing in your recommendation, is respecting the Driver's need to maintain his self-esteem. You are also allowing him to work in the independent way that he most enjoys. His self-respect is tied to his ability to make his own quality decisions. You are providing him with a means for doing this.

Asking for the Business

If you beat around the bush with the Driver customer, you just might not get the sale. You have got to ask him directly. You've given him the alternatives and allowed him to make a choice. Now it is time for him to buy—ask him for the sale. This is what he expects from you.

As with your recommendation, your offer should be put in clear terms. This way, the Driver will not have to waste his time with questions that should have been clearly answered in the offer. Of course, you include all the relevant facts. Nothing should be left open to question.

Even at this stage, you can offer more options if you feel that the Driver needs them. Since this customer must achieve his goals, he may feel more comfortable knowing that if Plan A doesn't work he can quickly shift to Plan B. He is a realist and knows that things can go wrong. He just wants to know that there are more than one means of getting things to go right.

Although the Driver may not do this in as detailed a manner as the Analytical, be prepared to deal with any changes he may make in the offer. The customer may attach conditions to the sale that you'll have to negotiate. In some cases this may seem like another indication of his need for power in your sales relationship; in others, it may be that he needs logical concessions from you. Either way, if you know that this can happen, you will have ready your own or your company's points for any negotiation.

At this point, the customer may need time to think over all the alternatives you have given him. Be patient. If he is truly interested, he will get back to you soon enough. He will want to get this purchase resolved.

By this time, you should know this customer's way of thinking about your product or service. While he's taking the time to go over your offer, you should come up with any objections that you think he might raise. In anticipation of having to deal with them when you get back together with the client, you can investigate any added information that you might need. Gather case histories, facts, examples, references, and anything else that will help you prepare to answer the Driver's objections.

Actually, his objections may be stated in broad terms. You will have to do more detective work and probe beyond the initial objections to get to the real facts of the matter. Doing this will put you in a better position to respond with information that is based on the Driver's own values and priorities.

Installing and Implementing the Solution

Finally, all of your homework has paid off. It's time to implement the solution. The Driver will be going full steam on the project and will expect you to do the same. Unless you set up a communication arrangement with this fast-moving customer, you may have trouble keeping track of what's going on.

A reasonable communication plan would be one that

encourages a quick exchange of information of what is happening on yours and his side. An easy guideline would be, say, to use natural checkpoints in the project as times for discussion. What has been accomplished so far, what progress has been made toward the larger goals would be topics to be covered.

Your having a contingency plan for this part of the process is a given. If anything disrupts the original implementation plan, you should be prepared to respond quickly. Your plan should include how you would have the problem corrected and how you could incorporate changes into the original plan without having to completely change it, which would be a great time-waster from the Driver's viewpoint.

Such a radical change from the Driver's original expectations would not, to say the least, be welcomed by him. The Driver customer does not appreciate such surprises. Besides the general confusion that this can cause, it also reflects poorly on his original decision—not a good thing for his self-esteem.

At this point, however, all of the background work that you have done in the earlier stages should have you prepared for anything that can happen now. If the Driver feels a sense of accomplishment—even though it may be with your help—you will have a very positive sales relationship with him.

SELLING TO EXPRESSIVE BUYERS

Yes, the Expressive buyer is Tell-Assertive, but remember that he is also Emote-Responsive. You can be friendlier with this buyer than you could be with the Driver. But just as they are more open, they are also more volatile. You will not get far by being reserved with this client. Enthusiasm counts.

Getting an Appointment

Expressives respond well to friendly introductory phone calls. Points for you to stress would be any quick benefits that this buyer will get from your product or service. He or she would also want to get to know you. What personal service will you offer? What is your experience? You might also answer a question about your company: What is your company's experience in dealing with its own products and services?

If it is not convenient for you to make an introductory phone call, you can write. In this case, your letter should be short and personal. Some of the points you'd cover would be the same as those in the phone call. Tell who you are, how you've heard of this Expressive customer, and what you're interested in discussing in your first meeting.

Opening the Call

The Expressive can be rather speedy, almost like the Driver. You have to keep up with him. Start out by quickly describing why you're making the sales call. Establish your business background so that the buyer will feel that you have credibility in the area that you are talking about. If the Expressive feels that you have earned your credentials, he'll think that you have the right to discuss business with him. This is the beginning of the sales relationship as he sees it.

You can take time—as much as you need—to share stories about people who you both know. The Expressive is certainly a people-oriented buyer. Discussing mutual acquaintances will give you a place in his "club." You can also share information with the Expressive that he might see as exclusive. He would like to know that you see him as an individual who's worthy of being singled out for important news.

Your tone should definitely be enthusiastic. That is, you should show enthusiasm for the Expressive's ideas. Feel free to share your positive feelings with him about his views. Show him that you really care about his goals. In your sales relationship with him, he will enjoy your participation in seeing to it that he gets what he wants.

With your competence established, the Expressive will be

more confident in dealing with you. Now is the time to develop an open and trusting personal relationship. As with the Amiable, the Expressive wants to get beyond the task discussions, and treat you like a friend. However, unlike the Amiable, the Expressive does not expect this to bouy up his own self-confidence. The Expressive has enough confidence on his own to get him through to a sales decision.

Discovering Buyer Needs

What is the Expressive's ideal outcome? If you can find this out, you will have a good beginning. What is his most perfect problem-solving vision?

While it is important to recognize that the Expressive is in fact self-confident in defining his own needs, he also can find it a pleasure to work with other people on this project. This could be a good place to bring other people into the process. Others who might contribute positively to the process are those who are a bit more analytical than the Expressive or those, like Drivers, who are better at following through with a straightforward plan.

Whoever else may come into the sales process, assuming that the Expressive is the ultimate buyer, it is up to you to listen to him. He is the one you are dealing with—at least, that's how he sees the situation. Be ready to respond to what you hear from him. He needs plenty of feedback, both verbal and nonverbal. He would like to hear from you that you support his ideas and beliefs.

This might be easier said than done. The Expressive is sometimes exploding with ideas. You could get a volley of them all at once. You might feel that some of them aren't necessarily connected to the others, or even to the business at hand. In other words, the Expressive can be a rambler at times—especially when he's excited about an idea.

In order to limit the rambling, you might ask questions. You need specific information in order to work productively on problem solving. Your questions should be concerned with getting answers to this critical data that you'll need when you make your recommendation.

Asking questions is one way to keep things in line. You will also have to be disciplined enough to keep yourself on track in the discussion. The Expressive can be very good at imaginative brainstorming. However, some ideas that come out of this type of session can cause your original plan to get out of focus. Try keeping the discussion as focused as possible so that you both can get to the immediate goal. This will help maintain progress in the sales relationship.

Reining the Expressive in may be a chore, especially if you've got to discuss specifics. Everyone knows that these things are important, it's just sometimes difficult for the Expressive to be interested in them. If you try to give a detailed account of pertinent information, you'll lose your buyer's attention. It will help both of you, however, if you take a break to summarize the specifics of what you've discussed. The points that you bring up in this summary should give direction to ways that both you and the buyer can progress toward making the Expressive's ideal vision a reality.

Making a Recommendation

Your summary should have given you a clearer notion of what the Expressive buyer needs. Now it's time to put your specific ideas for solutions to his problems in writing. Having the facts clearly written in black and white will help maintain focus in this important stage of the sales process. Too many details may prove overwhelming for the Expressive buyer. Give him enough to let him be confident that you have stated all the facts that you both need.

Even though you have stated the facts, you will need more time to discuss how your ideas might be implemented. Spend time discussing with the buyer the development of alternative plans. This brainstorming session should be more

focused that the first one because now you have actual well-defined plans and ideas to work with.

During these discussions, remember to show your respect for the Expressive in personal terms. Let him know that you appreciate the value of his ideas. This relationship-oriented buyer thrives on maintaining a high level of self-esteem. As long as that is intact, there should be no problem with maintaining a comfortable, productive tension zone.

On your side of the relationship, it will be best if you get any commitment from the Expressive in writing. Again, writing is a great tool for clarifying exactly whatever it is that the buyer is saying he will do. It is there, unquestionably, for both of you to see.

Asking for the Business

At some point, you'll have enough specific information about the buyer's needs. The time spent discussing how your recommendation can help the buyer should have shown him how appropriate it is for his situation. When you are comfortable that the customer is satisfied so far, you can assume that the sale is on its way to happening. Ask for the order casually, as informally as possible.

If you have the opportunity to do so, offer some incentive to the Expressive to buy. For instance, you can offer a price break or something value-added. This kind of incentive will add to the buyer's exclusive feeling about the purchase. This might add to the buyer's self-esteem, and to your ability to make the sale.

By now, you know that this customer carries a wealth of ideas just ready to be expressed. It would be to your advantage, at this point, not to unknowingly encourage more brainstorming by bringing up alternatives. Keep the important issues in line by not confusing things with more options. You want to keep things on a direct path to the signing of the purchase order.

One step toward getting this will be to ask for a definite commitment from the client. Again, this should be in writing.

Have the facts precisely spelled out—without excessive detail— so that the Expressive understands exactly what he is agreeing to buy.

When you have a firm purchasing decision from the Expressive, that's the time to deal with the details. Actually, you might discover that this buyer believes that it's your responsibility to handle the details of the agreement. So, you take care of them, but be sure that the customer adequately understands everything that is important in his purchase agreement.

If, at this stage, the Expressive still comes up with objections you can handle them on the personal level of your business relationship. For instance, you have already established mutual acquaintances. Use that information to show what these others have done to overcome a particular problem.

You can also continue to respond positively to the Expressive's enthusiasm. Describe to him how his purchase decision will help him reach his ideal goal. Even if this purchase will not get him directly to this goal, it should be a means for making progress toward his future accomplishment.

This buyer feels that his ideas and opinions are very important in getting to his objectives. In dealing with objections, you can discuss with him how your recommendation is in line with his own ideas, how it can lead his ideas to become realities.

Part of the Expressive's reality is the simple satisfaction of knowing that he made a good buying decision. Assure him that he is personally correct in choosing your product or service. Let him know the benefits that the decision will bring to all involved who are important to him.

Installing and Implementing the Purchase

Your personal business relationship with this buyer continues after the purchase order is signed. On the task side, you will have to make sure that the buyer understands the schedule for delivery and implementation. However, you should personally introduce the person or team that will do the implementation.

A very effective business follow-up with the Expressive buyer is for both of you to take part in a social situation. Going out to lunch can be a good opportunity for you both to deal with the Expressive's relationship-orientation needs as well as clear up any business issues that may be outstanding.

If the Expressive has any complaints about the implementation process, you should handle them yourself. This buyer might see it as a problem in your relationship if you referred his problems to someone else. If you must bring in someone with more specialized knowledge to help with the problem solving, make sure that you have the Expressive's permission to do so. In this case, it would be courteous for you to introduce the buyer and the specialist.

There's a good chance that the Expressive will see you as an ongoing member of his team if you continue to show respect for and interest in his achievement of his goals. Continuing with the relationship can be positive for both of you. You will be trusted, as a business friend, if the Expressive needs any further service or purchases.

Now that you have specific sales strategies for all the four social styles, in Chapter 11 we will bring things together. Having the strategies is not enough. Learning how to be versatile in your sales relationships will help you make any adjustments necessary for you to carry out these strategies. We'll discuss your ability to be versatile next.

11

Versatility:
How to Modify
Your Style

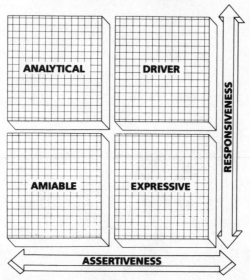

Remember that versatility is defined as the degree to which a salesperson is perceived as developing and maintaining buyer comfort throughout the sales process.

By now you know what the four social styles are, how people of each of these styles show tension and how you, the salesperson, can plan strategies to work with each of these styles. So, it should be clear: For you to be able to work productively with all of your customers, you must be versatile.

But how can you do this? You may have figured out that you are an Analytical. You just might think that Expressives are too scatterbrained. Or, if you are the Expressive, you might feel tense about the Analytical's nitpicking about details. Or the Driver might think the Amiable is too wishywashy. And the Amiable might be intimidated by the Driver's seeming impersonal approach. In other words, whatever you own style, you might have problems in dealing with others.

This is where versatility comes in. You know that in order to be a successful salesperson you will have to get along with all of your clients. Even if they don't all buy every proposal you offer, you'll want to create a good impression. If they can't use your product or service now, they might want to call on you in the future, and they might have friends who will need your product now.

You might also want to enjoy your work. That would surely be difficult to achieve if you feel tension with three out of four of your customers. Your versatility will help you to keep your sales relationships in the productive tension zone. The comfortable area for all involved.

Remember that versatility is defined as *the degree to which a salesperson is perceived as developing and maintaining buyer comfort throughout the sales process.* This does not mean that you become another person or give up who you are. You should always maintain your own integrity, especially with what you do best. The main reason for your being versatile is to keep the buyer's comfort level high.

The customer will not feel very comfortable if you attempt to impose your own social style on him. As we've seen in backup behavior, the buyer who feels this will often times be confused, feel unproductive tension, and have unmet expectations. All of which you would like to avoid. It is much better to temporarily adjust your behavior to fit the buyer's style. Both of you will feel more comfortable.

Versatility, then, is not like social style. Social style stays very much the same. You might be able to modify yours slightly, say, move from one subquadrant to another within one style. To completely change your social style, however, is extremely difficult to do. You would have to change the responses you learned as a child, your attitudes toward work and relationships, and just about everything else that you know as "you."

On the other hand, versatility can be learned. You can increase yours quite a bit by practice and training. Beware, though, if you choose not to be versatile or if you're just not concerned about it, you can lose your ability to get along comfortably with other social styles. So it pays to use what you learn.

THE VERSATILITY SCALE

You will find that versatility isn't static. There are degrees of it. The fact that some people are more versatile than others can be visualized by placement on a scale (Exhibit 1).

On the left side of this scale—the areas with letters W and X—are those people who are perceived as not adapting their behavior to help others feel comfortable. That is, they are

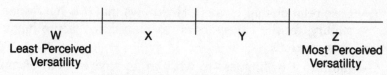

Exhibit 1   The Versatility Scale

perceived as having a lower degree of versatility. For example, a salesperson with lower versatility may be seen by his customers as

- Doing business in his own self-interest. He may appear to be more interested in making the sale and enriching his own bank account than he is in sincerely helping the customer solve his problems.
- Behaving in a style that is mainly comfortable for himself. The customer may feel that the salesperson doesn't care enough about him to be concerned about his needs.
- Consequently, running the risk of creating relationship tension and undue discomfort for the buyer in the sales situation. There is the possibility the both the salesperson and the customer will go to backup behavior.

On the other side of the scale—the Y and Z areas—are those persons perceived as adapting their behavior to help others feel comfortable. They show a higher degree of perceived versatility. The behavior of a salesperson with a higher degree of versatility would

- Appear to be flexible and adaptive. He would know how to adjust his presentation for customers of each social style.
- Encourage communication with people of styles other than his own. He would not seek out like-minded customers. Instead, he would enlarge his potential customer base by working with all styles.

- Ease relationship tension. He knows that it is his responsibility, as the salesperson, to maintain the productive tension zone.
- Indicate a willingness to work in an environment of mutual understanding and cooperation. He recognizes back-up behavior and is able to draw out problems early so that they do not become overwhelming later.

Even within each quartile on the scale, there is great variation in versatility among people. Developing your sensitivity to these differences will go a long way to increase your success in the sales situation. You can begin to be more versatile by extending yourself to help the buyer feel more comfortable.

This is your goal as a versatile salesperson. You will want to be able to apply what you know about social styles to the day-to-day sales process. This means that you will have to be ready and able to quickly adapt your behavior to your customer's expectations. If your Amiable buyer wants more time to develop the sales relationship, you, the Driver, will be able to adjust your task orientation to do so.

Awareness of what the buyer wants—no matter what his social style may be—is a skill that's definitely worth developing. Understanding buyer needs will give you insights into what you should do to keep the buyer's comfort zone in balance. Many times, when the customer realizes that you are working to make him feel comfortable, he will try doing the same for you. This will lead to a very effective sales relationship.

TECHNIQUES FOR STYLE MODIFICATION

Practice in working with customers of different social styles will improve your skills. Things will come easier for you as your degree of versatility improves. "Style Modification" is a way to increase your versatility.

Style modification is temporarily adjusting your assertiveness and/or responsiveness to encourage others to interact productively with you.

Do you find that too often, you tend to act in ways that are most comfortable for you? That is, do you follow your own social style. By doing this you are able to stay within your own comfort zone. This, however, is not the most effective way to work with customers because you will limit yourself to your own needs and not those of others. Staying within your own comfort zone can cause your clients to feel tension or general discomfort.

Now that you know about social styles, with practice, you should be able to understand what the customer wants from you. You know how he expects to be treated. If you can put yourself in his shoes, you will get a feeling for what his expectations are. With this knowledge you will be able to adapt your own behavior to meet the client's needs.

The key here is *empathy*. Your ability to feel empathy with the customer will determine how versatile you are. This is what will tell you how to modify your social style in every sales relationship.

Remember that you are only temporarily modifying your behavior. You are not becoming a different person by completely changing your social style. You are simply adjusting your responsiveness and/or your assertiveness in order to work in the productive tension zone with your customer.

An example of this kind of modification with opposite social styles could be the interaction of a Driving Driver salesperson and an Amiable Amiable customer. The Driver will want to get things done quickly and effectively in a controlled manner. This particular Driver is highly task oriented.

On the other hand, the Amiable needs a lot of time to get to know the salesperson. He wants to develop a personal relationship so that he can feel better about, or trust, the sales process. He is highly responsive to others while the Driver is not.

In order to work effectively with the Amiable customer, the Driver salesperson should temporarily adjust both his assertiveness and his responsiveness. He can do this by decreasing his assertiveness—the Amiable will feel more comfortable if the Driver does not come on too strong. He can also increase his responsiveness by showing the Amiable that he does care about the personal aspects of the sales relationship.

Of course, the Driver in this case will be temporarily postponing the needs of his own social style. However, he will have the bonus of being able to encourage the Amiable to work with him.

When you find yourself in a sales relationship with a customer who appears to demonstrate your own style, you should consider style modification on your part. Very often difficulties can arise because both people have the same needs. There can be a clash of wills here.

For example, suppose you are an Expressive and you meet an Expressive customer. Both of you are Emote-Responsive and Tell-Assertive. Also, both of you enjoy dominating the sales situation.

In this case, the salesperson should reduce his assertiveness. This way, he allows the customer to keep most of the spotlight in the relationship. The salesperson, however, uses his responsive behavior—a quality that the Expressive customer enjoys in others. This modification will keep the sales process in the comfort zone.

A Driver salesperson says that, when he works with other Drivers, he too must decrease his assertiveness. Otherwise, all involved with the project will want to be chiefs. The problem with this is that since they cannot all be in control, those who aren't will find ways to exert their control in other ways, or simply refuse to play the game. Obviously, the project won't work this way. So, for him, it has been a matter of learning how to follow when the situation calls for it. By using this versatility skill, his Driver's need for task completion ultimately happens.

You are not simply left to your feelings about the situation when it comes to style modification. There are many specific things that you can learn to do to adjust your own style to the needs of others. Exhibit 2 lists some guidelines for style modification. What follows are some of the most important suggestions for you to practice.

Increasing Assertiveness

Appearing to be more Tell-Assertive could be a concern of Analyticals and Amiables in sales. This is particularly true for if you are a salesperson who would like to be perceived as actually having the authority that you can rightfully claim to have. Increasing your assertiveness will have a positive impact in your sales relationships.

Generally, you will want to tell more and ask less. Here are some suggestions to help you adjust your social style in the sales process.

- *Get to the point.* Ask-Assertives tend to ramble at times. They can be vague and even ambiguous with customers. Many clients are really put off by this kind of behavior—even if you are doing this with the purpose of appearing tactful. The buyer wants to know specifically what it is that you are discussing. So, say what you mean in direct language. Let the buyer know exactly where you stand. You can do this by simplifying your statements. The buyer will get a much clearer understanding of your ideas.

- *Volunteer information.* Learn to turn what you would normally phrase as questions into statements. Be forthright with your opinions. Take the lead yourself. Don't wait for others. You'll be much more effective in the sales relationship if you come straight out with your ideas.

- *Be willing to disagree.* Ask-Assertives can be very supportive of other people's ideas in their sales relationships. Because of this, you may many times find it difficult to

Increasing Responsiveness

Central   **Emote** a little more often.
Theme   **Control** a little less often.

How to Increase Responsiveness
1. Verbalize feelings.
2. Pay personal compliments.
3. Be willing to spend time on the relationship.
4. Engage in small talk—socialize.
5. Use more friendly, nonverbal language.

Increasing Assertiveness

Central   **Tell** a little
Theme   more often.
           Ask a little less often.

How to Increase Assertiveness
1. Get to the point.
2. Volunteer information.
3. Be willing to disagree.
4. Act on your convictions.
5. Initiate conversation.

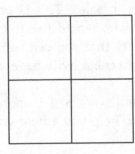

Decreasing Assertiveness

Central   **Ask** a little
Theme   more often.
           Tell a little less often.

How to Decrease Assertiveness
1. Ask for opinions of others.
2. Negotiate decision-making.
3. Listen without interrupting.
4. Adapt to time needs of others.
5. Allow others to assume leadership more often.

Decreasing Responsiveness

Central   **Control** a little more often.
Theme   **Emote** a little less often.

How to Decrease Responsiveness
1. Talk less.
2. Restrain your enthusiasm.
3. Make decisions based on facts.
4. Stop and think.
5. Acknowledge the thoughts of others.

Exhibit 2   Guidelines for Style Modification

disagree with your clients. Keep in mind, though, that if you want to appear to be an effective problem-solver, there will be times when you will have to disagree with the buyer. The best thing to do is not to worry when your most reasonable comments conflict with the buyer's point of view. Learn how to disagree without becoming defensive or personally involved.

- *Act on your convictions.* This is especially valuable when you work with Expressive or Driver clients. If you avoid issues with them, you can create a lot of tension. Learn to be decisive. Be able to take a firm stand. These buyers will have much more respect for you.
- *Initiate conversation.* Instead of waiting to respond to others' ideas, take the lead yourself. Introduce your ideas and sales solutions. Yes, this may, at times, seem risky to you, but look at it this way. If you don't speak up you may be depriving your customers of your valuable input. You will increase your effectiveness by contributing and sharing your ideas in the sales process.

Decreasing Assertiveness

Expressives and Drivers can have just the opposite problem. They may be seen as too pushy by their clients. As was mentioned for the Ask-Assertives, it is true that you should have some assertiveness to be effective as a salesperson. However, if you have too much, you will find that your buyers will resist you. In other words, you could lose sales. This can be especially true when you meet with Amiables and Analyticals. Try cutting back on your need to control. Respond more to others' needs. Here are some ideas on how you can tone down your assertiveness when it's necessary in the sales process.

- *Ask for the opinion of others.* As a Tell-Assertive you probably have many good ideas on what the customer needs. Of course, you want to let him know what your ideas are. There are times, however, when the only way you will really know what the client wants is to ask him questions. Asking him what his needs are is usually more productive than your attempting to tell him. Allow him to take part in the discussion of solutions to his problem. That way he will get only what he wants and will not get unacceptable products or services that you think he should have.

- *Negotiate decision making.* You will have to do a little more than just allow the customer to speak. You should be able to acknowledge that the buyer's point of view can be vital to good communication in the sales relationship. The customer is expressing his personal ideas and feelings in the discussion. Listen to him, and respond to his feelings as well as his facts.

- *Listen without interrupting.* Fast-paced Drivers and Expressives tend to become impatient with others who they perceive as slower in expressing their ideas, or those who discuss points that the Tell-Assertives think of as irrelevant. Try to be more patient. Don't interrupt or disregard this customer. Listening patiently to others is a good way to decrease assertiveness.

- *Adapt to the time needs of others.* Learn how to pace yourself in the sales process. A good sense of timing is as important in the sales environment as a sense of urgency. Be sensitive to the fact that your buyer may need more time to grasp an idea or think it through. Your being able to adapt can be very rewarding in solving both relationship and task problems.

- *Allow buyers to assume leadership more often.* Tell-Assertives are more often than not take-charge people. This leadership ability certainly has its place. However, some of your customers may resent it. They may think that you're infringing on their territory or putting their executive authority in question. Allow your clients to determine the agenda or direction of the discussion. This can go a long way in reducing a high level of assertiveness.

Decreasing Responsiveness

Emote-Responsive Amiable and Expressive salespeople very often need to control their emotions in the business environment. Without this control, buyers may perceive these salespeople as being too emotionally involved in the sales process. That is, their approach may seem to be overly subjective. This style of selling that is more feeling than fact will make it more difficult to reach objective sales goals.

To appear more businesslike, work at developing a manner that suggests a serious approach without being cold or indifferent. This means that you'll be controlling more and emoting less. This is a good skill to have when you work with Analyticals and Drivers. Here are some suggestions on how you can do this.

- *Talk less.* Emote-Responsive salespeople enjoy talking, sometimes even monopolizing the conversation. Some buyers may appreciate this, others do not. Listen more and talk less. This will increase your effectiveness with buyers who are less responsive than you.

- *Restrain your enthusiasm.* Calm down your display of feelings. Too much of this can strike some customers as immature behavior on your part. The best way to influence buyers is to show balance and self-control throughout the sales process.

- *Make decisions based on facts.* Do you have a tendency to make judgments based on "gut feelings" rather than facts? If you do, Drivers and Analyticals can have problems working with you. They prefer more rational decision making. Learn to explain your sales recommendations by emphasizing facts to gain the approval of these buyers.

- *Stop and think.* Guard against being impulsive and hasty. Learning to pause for a moment to reflect before speaking or acting can help keep your responsiveness in check.

- *Acknowledge the thoughts of buyers.* Zero in on the needs and expectations of your customers. If you show too much responsiveness, the focus will be on you instead of the buyer. Always recognize that your clients may have good ideas, too, and deserve the opportunity to make them known.

Increasing Responsiveness

Analytical and Driver salespeople, in particular, should work at emoting more often and controlling less. It's true that businesslike behavior does call for some restraint. Moderate reserve indicates to others a seriousness of purpose, a certain maturity.

Too much restraint, however, makes it difficult for you to relate to your customers. They may see you as cold, impersonal and even hard-hearted. You may be perceived as being either unable or unwilling to be warm and understanding toward your customers. This can be especially true when you work with Amiable and Expressive buyers. The following are some skills that you'll find useful in dealing with your clients.

- *Verbalize feelings.* Suppressing your emotions does not improve communication. Speak up and admit to your emotions. You may be surprised to find that the sales relationship may actually improve if you open up and let your feelings be known.

- *Pay personal compliments.* Your sincere compliments given to deserving clients are always welcome. Don't hesitate to express your good sentiments. Simply not stating a negative comment about a customer is not enough. Let him know your positive feelings. You can also find indirect ways to pay compliments. That is, you can remember a client's birthday, write him a letter, ask him about his family members or his social activities.

- *Be willing to spend time on relationships.* Of course, personal involvement does not always lead directly to the achievement of your sales goals. Your ability to show friendship and sensitivity to the feelings of others can, however, certainly enrich your sales relationships. It can also build feelings of loyalty and cooperation on both sides of the relationship—yours as well as the customer's. Rather than reject them, let your feelings enter into the relationship in a balanced and appropriate way. Learn to look at the feeling side of human nature.

- *Engage in small talk—socialize.* One way of being more responsive is to take the time to make pleasant social small talk. You can, in fact, mix this kind of communication with your more goal-oriented conversation. Naturally, you should engage in social conversations that have nothing to do with business, at the appropriate times. Buyers, like most other people, appreciate your dealing with them on the personal level as much as they appreciate your accepting them as an equal in the sales relationship.
- *Use more friendly and nonverbal language.* Relax— especially in your speech and body language. Although there will always be some more reserved buyers who will disapprove, most of your customers will enjoy your relaxed manner. Usually you can help your clients feel more comfortable when you use informal language and casual gestures.

ADDING BALANCE TO YOUR SOCIAL STYLE

As you've seen, each social style has its own strengths and weaknesses. What's interesting about it is that each style tends to be weak in an area where its opposite—the style diagonally across the matrix—has its greatest strengths. For instance, the Driver needs the ability to listen—something the Amiable has plenty of. The Amiable, however, need the ability to act decisively—something the Driver excels in.

You can add balance to your own social style by learning to adjust your assertiveness and responsiveness. This will help you to maintain a comfort zone with your buyers, no matter what their style may be. Here are some suggestions for adding balance to the four social styles.

- *Amiables need to initiate.* Amiables are inclined to spend more time and energy on developing the relationship than working at the task at hand. This is because of their need for acceptance by others. If you are an Amiable, learn that your own self-esteem and the acceptance and esteem of others can be won by initiating and then working towards the progress of accomplishing to goals of the task. Try adding balance to your style by simply getting started. Set goals and then decisively follow through.

- *Analyticals need to act.* Analyticals can become more confident by taking calculated risks. Since your action is based on careful research, the odds for succeeding are in your favor. Don't fall into the trap of waiting to complete a task because you think that you need more facts. Trust your own good judgment and go ahead with the project.
- *Drivers need to listen.* You are goal-oriented and believe that you are capable of reaching your objective by using your own resources. Your independence is based on your own needs and perceptions. Try allowing others to have input in the progress of the task. There are times when others can help you reach your goals more effectively than you can alone. By listening and acting on the ideas, feelings and needs of others, your project can take on a new, more balanced dimension.
- *Expressives need to check.* Expressives like to work in fast-moving, stimulating settings with energetic people. At times, this can get you carried away and you can lose sight of your immediate objectives. You can avoid this if you pay more attention to details. Ask yourself what could be the consequences of your actions. Do this, and you will find yourself gaining self-discipline, as well as the admiration of others.

Now you have it—a good understanding of just what it takes to be a versatile salesperson. An Expressive-Expressive salesperson has used the concepts that you've learned to both work more effectively with her clients and to modify her own social style to add balance in her sales relationships. For instance, she had been having a lot of difficulty in dealing with a particular Analytical customer. She felt that she never had enough information for him. The more she had, the more he wanted. The whole sales process was becoming increasingly frustrating for all involved. He constantly complained and she dreaded making her sales calls.

When she learned about versatility, she was able to understand what this client needed. She realized that it might be difficult for her to work with this customer alone because of the difference in the needs of the two social styles. She did as much as she could herself, and also brought in a partner—an Analytical salesperson—to some of the meetings with this client. She was able to maintain control and satisfy the customer's need for more details. Even without her associate, her sales relationship with this buyer prospered.

She also realized that an Expressive-Expressive social style just might be a bit overwhelming for most of her customers. She wanted to appear more businesslike. For this, the style modification techniques came in handy. She is now perceived to be a Driving Expressive—a good balance of task- and relationship-oriented behavior. Notice that she did not radically change her social style. She simply adjusted her behavior to make her customers more comfortable.

Now it's your turn. You have all you need to bring a very positive dimension to your sales relationships. Practice being more versatile. To get you started, give some thought to the "Sales Strategy Planning Sheet" in the Appendix. It will pay in sales and friendships, many times over. Also, for your convenience, in the Appendix you will find a summary of how you should approach and sell buyers of each of the four social styles.

Appendix A

Impact of Social Style on Customers

SUCCESSFUL SALE

Think about your relationship to a customer in a recently completed *successful* sale.

1. How might your own social style have had a positive effect on this customer?

_____

_____

_____

_____

_____

_____

_____

_____

_____

_____

_____

2. How might your own style have had a negative effect on this customer?

_____

_____

_____

_____

_____

_____

_____

_____

_____

_____

_____

UNSUCCESSFUL SALE

Think about your relationship to a customer in a recently attempted *unsuccessful* sale.

1. How might your own social style have had a positive effect on this customer?

_____

_____

_____

_____

_____

_____

_____

_____

_____

_____

_____

2. How might your own style have had a negative effect on this customer?

_____

_____

_____

_____

_____

_____

_____

_____

_____

_____

_____

SUMMARY

1. How may your social style be helping your sales?

_____

_____

_____

_____

_____

_____

_____

_____

_____

_____

2. How may your social style be hindering your sales?

_____

_____

_____

_____

_____

_____

_____

_____

_____

_____

Appendix B

Social Style Identification

Social style evaluator

Name of prospect: _____ Date _____

I would describe this person as: (Circle the appropriate letter/number.)

Following......Taking charge	Cool................Warm
D C B A	1 2 3 4
Quiet.............. Talkative	Calm..............Excitable
D C B A	1 2 3 4
Go-along.......Challenging	Reserved.............. Open
D C B A	1 2 3 4
Passive...........Dominant	Task-oriented. People-oriented
D C B A	1 2 3 4
Asking.............. Stating	Poker-faced........Animated
D C B A	1 2 3 4
Cooperative..... Competitive	Aloof..............Intimate
D C B A	1 2 3 4
Introverted....... Extroverted	Inward............Outgoing
D C B A	1 2 3 4
Slow, studied......Fast-paced	Controlled........ Emotional
D C B A	1 2 3 4
Unassertive........ Assertive	Hard to read.... Easy to read
D C B A	1 2 3 4
Indecisive..........Decisive	Unresponsive......Responsive
D C B A	1 2 3 4

Total: _____ _____ _____ _____   _____ _____ _____ _____

Compute the totals of each column. The letter and the number with the highest scores give you the best indications of your prospect's assertiveness and responsiveness.

I believe this person's social style to be: _____

Social style evaluator

Name of prospect: _____ Date _____

I would describe this person as: (Circle the appropriate letter/number.)

Following......Taking charge	Cool...................Warm
D C B A	1 2 3 4
Quiet.............. Talkative	Calm...............Excitable
D C B A	1 2 3 4
Go-along ....Challenging	Reserved.............. Open
D C B A	1 2 3 4
Passive ....Dominant	Task-oriented. People-oriented
D C B A	1 2 3 4
Asking .... Stating	Poker-faced ....Animated
D C B A	1 2 3 4
Cooperative..... Competitive	Aloof............... Intimate
D C B A	1 2 3 4
Introverted....... Extroverted	Inward .... Outgoing
D C B A	1 2 3 4
Slow, studied......Fast-paced	Controlled .... Emotional
D C B A	1 2 3 4
Unassertive .... Assertive	Hard to read .... Easy to read
D C B A	1 2 3 4
Indecisive...........Decisive	Unresponsive......Responsive
D C B A	1 2 3 4

Total: _____ _____ _____ _____   _____ _____ _____ _____

Compute the totals of each column. The letter and the number with the highest scores give you the best indications of your prospect's assertiveness and responsiveness.

I believe this person's social style to be: _____

Appendix C

Strategy for Selling

Selling to the Analytical Buyer

Getting an Appointment

1. First send a businesslike letter which provides:
   - product/service information which addresses details and specifics
   - details about yourself and your company
   - your professional credentials
   - reference to a third-party success

   Stress how your product works, how it will be cost effective, your stability, and your experience.

2. Follow the letter with a phone call in which you confirm expectations about the duration and outcome of the first meeting.

Opening the Call

1. Do not underestimate the need to provide background information about you, your company, and your expertise.

2. Approach this buyer in an advisory capacity; acknowledge the Analytical's "expert" status.

3. Show evidence that you have done your homework on the buyer's situation and possible needs.

4. Offer evidence of situations where your problem-solving resulted in solutions to business problems.

5. Be conscious of how you are using the Analytical's time.

Discovering Buyer Needs

1. Ask specific, fact-finding questions. Consider the buyer in an organized, systematic manner, leading to a comprehensive exchange of information.

2. Attempt to balance the factual information by encouraging the Analytical to discuss ideas and feelings.

3. Be thorough and unhurried. Be prepared to listen to more than you want to know.

4. Indicate to Analytical buyers that you are in alignment with their thinking and can support their objectives.

5. Keep in mind that a comprehensive discovery process with Analyticals will pay off when you need to justify your recommendations and handle objections from this buyer.

Making a Recommendation

1. Provide a detailed written proposal of your recommendation, but make sure that you present it to the Analytical in person.

2. Make sure your proposal includes the strongest possible cost justification. Clearly present all numbers and how you arrived at them.

3. Make your presentation organized, systematic, and precise.

4. If you cannot answer a specific question, offer to find out the answer, and get back to the Analytical with it.

5. Be reserved but not cold; decisive but not aggressive.

6. Limit use of emotional appeals or "who else is doing it" as evidence.

7. Recommend a specific course of action.

8. Give the buyer the opportunity to review all documents related to purchase and delivery.

Asking for the Business

1. Ask for the order directly, but in a low-key way.

2. Expect to negotiate changes on details in standard paperwork; think through and be ready with the details.

3. Pay special attention to pricing issues.

4. Work for a commitment **now** to avoid the Analytical's tendency to delay or to ask for more data later.

5. Cite data which stresses your company's record and service capabilities.

6. When answering objections, respond to the Analytical's buying principles and objectivity.

Installing/Implementing

1. Provide a detailed implementation plan which establishes:
    - your responsibilities
    - the buyer's responsibilities
    - a schedule for implementation (such as a PERT chart)
    - the implementation procedure.

2. Maintain periodic, regular contact with the Analytical buyer, checking to see that implementation is satisfactory and on schedule.

Selling to the Driver Buyer

Getting an Appointment

1. Drivers may not take time to read an introductory letter.

   You may prefer to make your first contact by phone, followed by a letter. The phone call to the Driver should be businesslike and to the point. Take only enough time to identify yourself, explain the business problem your product/service addresses, and ask for an appointment.

2. The letter should confirm the time and date of the appointment and include materials the Driver may ask to review prior to the meeting.

Opening the Call

1. Provide knowledge and insight to solving a specific business problem.

2. Listen and focus complete attention on the Driver's ideas and objectives.

3. Be personable, but reserved and relatively formal.

4. Present factual evidence which establishes the business problem and resulting outcome.

5. Maintain a quick pace. Drivers value punctuality and efficient use of their time.

Discovering Buyer Needs

1. Ask, don't tell. Ask fact-finding questions leading to what the Driver values and rewards.

2. Clarify priorities.

3. Make your line of questioning consistent with your call objective.

4. Follow up on requests for information immediately.

5. Support the buyer's beliefs; indicate how you can positively impact goals.

6. Clarify the Driver's expectation of the next step.

Making a Recommendation

1. Present your recommendation so that the Driver can compare alternative solutions and their probable outcomes.

2. Provide documented options.

3. Offer the best quality given the cost limitations.

4. Be specific and factual without overwhelming with details.

5. Appeal to esteem and independence needs; reinforce the Driver's preference for acting in a forthright manner.

6. Summarize content quickly, then let the Driver choose a course of action.

Asking for the Business

1. Ask for the order directly; don't beat around the bush.

2. Put your offer in clear, factual terms.

3. Offer options and alternatives.

4. Be prepared to negotiate changes and concessions. Drivers sometimes attach conditions to a sale.

5. Offer the Driver time to consider the options.

6. Anticipate objections in advance; come prepared with facts, examples, case histories, or references to answer those objections.

7. Probe beyond initial objections to get the facts; then respond to objections based on the Driver's values and priorities.

Installing/Implementing

1. Set up a communication arrangement with the Driver which encourages quick exchange of information about checkpoints and milestones.

2. Make sure you have a contingency plan to responsively implement corrections and incorporate changes.

3. Make sure there are no surprises.

Selling to the Expresive Buyer

Getting an Appointment

1. Generally a phone call is most appropriate. Make it open and friendly, stressing quick benefits, personal service, your experience, and your company's experience with its products/services.

2. If you decide to write a letter, make it short and personal, telling:
   - who you are
   - how you know of the Expressive
   - what you're interested in talking about.

Opening the Call

1. Quickly describe the purpose of your call and establish credibility. You must earn the right to develop a business relationship with the Expressive.

2. Share stories about people you both know.

3. Share information the Expressive would perceive as exclusive.

4. Share your feelings and enthusiasm for the Expressive's ideas and goals.

5. Once the Expressive has confidence in your competence, take time to develop an open and trusting personal relationship.

Discovering Buyer Needs

1. Begin by finding out the Expressive's vision of the ideal outcome.

2. Identify other people who should contribute to analysis and planning.

3. Listen, then respond with plenty of verbal and nonverbal feedback that supports the Expressive's beliefs.

4. Question carefully for the critical data you'll need.

5. Keep the discussion focused and moving toward a result.

6. If the Expressive shows limited interest in specifics, summarize what has been discussed and begin to suggest ways to move the vision toward reality.

Making a Recommendation

1. Provide specific solutions to the Expressive's ideas, in writing. Build confidence that you have the necessary facts, but don't overwhelm the Expressive with details.

2. Don't rush the discussion — spend time developing ways to implement ideas.

3. Appeal to personal esteem needs.

4. Try to get commitments to action in writing.

Asking for the Business

1. When you have enough information about needs and have tested the appropriateness of the recommendation, assume the sale and ask for the order in a casual, informal way.

2. When the opportunity presents itself, offer a price break, something value-added, or other incentives to encourage the purchase.

3. Don't confuse the issue with options.

4. Get a definite commitment; be sure the Expressive understands the decision to buy.

5. Save the details until after you have a firm buying decision. The Expressive believes it is the salesperson's job to handle details.

6. In handling objections:
    *   describe what others have done to get over that hurdle
    *   respond to the Expressive's enthusiasm for his/her goals
    *   deal with how the recommendation meets with this buyer's opinions
    *   restate benefits that focus on the satisfaction a buying decision will bring.

Installing/Implementing

1. As soon as the purchase order is signed, reaffirm the schedule for delivery and your personal relationship with the buyer, and introduce the implementation person or team.

2. A social situation such as lunch can be a very effective opportunity for following up on business with this buyer.

3. Work toward becoming an ongoing member of the buyer's team.

4. In case of any complaints, handle them yourself. Never refer them to another in your organization without the buyer's assent.

Selling to the Amiable Buyer

Getting an Appointment

1. Send a letter with a personal touch, stating who you are, and why you are contacting the Amiable. Stress the following:
   - your experience working with clients the Amiable knows by reputation or experience
   - your reliability and follow-through
   - the quality of your product/service

2. Follow your letter with a personal phone call. Take time to be friendly, open, honest, sincere, and to establish trust in the relationship.

Opening the Call

1. Engage in informal conversation before getting down to business.

2. Demonstrate that you are personally interested in the Amiable's work and personal goals. You will have to earn the right to learn more personally about the Amiable.

3. Demonstrate your product/service knowledge by referencing a common acquaintance with whom you've done business.

Discovering Buyer Needs

1. Create a cooperative atmosphere with an open exchange of information and feelings.

2. Amiables tend to understate their objectives, so you may need to question them on specifics for achieving their long-term goals.

3. Listen responsively. Give plenty of verbal and nonverbal feedback.

4. Verify whether there are unresolved budget or cost justification issues.

5. Find out who else will contribute to the buying decision.

6. Summarize what you believe to be the Amiable's key ideas and feelings.

Making a Recommendation

1. Define clearly in writing and make sure the Amiable understands:
   - what you can and will do to support the Amiable's personal goals
   - what you will contribute and what the Amiable needs to contribute
   - the support resources you intend to commit to the project.

2. Provide a clear solution to the Amiable's problem with maximum assurance that this is the best solution and there is no need to consider others.

3. Ask the Amiable to involve the ultimate decision maker.

4. Satisfy safety needs by:
   - showing how your solution is best now and will be best in the future
   - using references and third-party evidence.

Asking for the Business

1. Ask for the order indirectly. Don't push.

2. Emphasize guarantees — how the Amiable is protected.

3. Don't corner Amiables; they want a way out if things go wrong.

4. Guard against "buyers' remorse" — get a commitment even if you have to base it on a contingency.

5. Stress your personal involvement in following up on the order.

6. Encourage the Amiable to involve others in the final buying decision.

7. Welcome objections, and be patient and thorough in answering them.

8. When answering objections:
    • describe financial justification
    • refer to experts, or other people the Amiable respects
    • keep in mind how the Amiable feels about and will be affected by the buying decision.

Installing/Implementing

1. Immediately after purchase order is signed, make an appointment to outline matters such as:
    • congratulating the Amiable on the buying decision
    • providing an implementation plan and schedule of events
    • arranging satisfactory payment schedules.

2. Thereafter, initiate and maintain frequent contacts providing services such as these:
    • periodic progress reports on installation
    • arrangements for service and training
    • introduction of new services
    • listening carefully to concerns, even those which seem trivial

Appendix D
Social Style Summary

	ANALYTICAL	AMIABLE	DRIVER	EXPRESSIVE
PRIMARY ASSET	Systematic	Supportive	Controlling	Energizing
BACKUP BEHAVIOR	Avoidance	Acquiescence	Autocratic	Attacking
FOR GROWTH NEEDS TO	Decide	Initiate	Listen	Check
MEASURE OF PERSONAL VALUE	Respect	Approval	Power	Recognition
NEEDS CLIMATE THAT	Describes	Processes	Responds	Collaborates
LET THEM SAVE	Face	Relationships	Time	Effort
MAKE EFFORT TO BE	Accurate	Cooperative	Efficient	Interesting
SUPPORT THEIR	Principles and Thinking	Relationships and Feelings	Conclusions and Actions	Visions and Intuitions
STRESS BENEFITS THAT ANSWER	HOW problem is solved	WHY solution is best	WHAT solution will do	WHO else has used
MAKE SURE SALES PROPOSAL EMPHASIZES	Evidence & Service	Assurances & Guarantees	Options & Probabilities	Testimony & Incentives
FOLLOW-UP WITH	Service	Support	Results	Attention

Appendix E

Sales Strategy
Planning Sheet

Buyer's Name: _____

I perceive this buyer's social style to be: _____

I perceive this buyer's versatility to be: ____ W   ____ X   ____ Y   ____ Z

My social style and versatility are: _____ / ___ W   ___ X   ___ Y   ___ Z

General Strategy

Based on my social style and my perception of the social style of this person, I plan to:

     ____ Increase assertiveness   ____ Increase responsiveness

     ____ Decrease assertiveness   ____ Decrease responsiveness

     ____ Not change assertiveness   ____ Not change responsiveness

In general, I plan to modify my style by:

_____

_____

_____

Specific Strategy

My specific sales strategy for each phase of the sales process will be:

1. Getting an
   Appointment

2. Opening
   the Call

3. Discovering
   Buyer Needs

4. Making a
   Recommendation

5. Asking for
   the Business

6. Installing and
   Implementing

Buyer's Name: _____

I perceive this buyer's social style to be: _____

I perceive this buyer's versatility to be: ___ W   ___ X   ___ Y   ___ Z

My social style and versatility are: _____ / ___ W   ___ X   ___ Y   ___ Z

General Strategy

Based on my social style and my perception of the social style of this person, I plan to: ·

    ___ Increase assertiveness   ___ Increase responsiveness

    ___ Decrease assertiveness   ___ Decrease responsiveness

    ___ Not change assertiveness   ___ Not change responsiveness

In general, I plan to modify my style by:

_____

_____

_____

Specific Strategy

My specific sales strategy for each phase of the sales process will be:

1. Getting an   _____
   Appointment

                   _____

2. Opening   _____
   the Call

                   _____

3. Discovering   _____
   Buyer Needs

                   _____

4. Making a   _____
   Recommendation

                   _____

5. Asking for   _____
   the Business

                   _____

6. Installing and   _____
   Implementing

                   _____

Buyer's Name: _____

I perceive this buyer's social style to be: _____

I perceive this buyer's versatility to be: ___ W   ___ X   ___ Y   ___ Z

My social style and versatility are: _____ / ___ W   ___ X   ___ Y   ___ Z

General Strategy

Based on my social style and my perception of the social style of this person, I plan to:

___ Increase assertiveness   ___ Increase responsiveness

___ Decrease assertiveness   ___ Decrease responsiveness

___ Not change assertiveness   ___ Not change responsiveness

In general, I plan to modify my style by:

_____

_____

_____

Specific Strategy

My specific sales strategy for each phase of the sales process will be:

1. Getting an
   Appointment   _____

                          _____

2. Opening
   the Call   _____

                          _____

3. Discovering
   Buyer Needs   _____

                          _____

4. Making a
   Recommendation   _____

                          _____

5. Asking for
   the Business   _____

                          _____

6. Installing and
   Implementing   _____

                          _____

Buyer's Name: _____

I perceive this buyer's social style to be: _____

I perceive this buyer's versatility to be: ___ W   ___ X   ___ Y   ___ Z

My social style and versatility are: _____ / ___ W   ___ X   ___ Y   ___ Z

General Strategy

Based on my social style and my perception of the social style of this person, I plan to: ·

___ Increase assertiveness   ___ Increase responsiveness

___ Decrease assertiveness   ___ Decrease responsiveness

___ Not change assertiveness   ___ Not change responsiveness

In general, I plan to modify my style by:

_____

_____

_____

Specific Strategy

My specific sales strategy for each phase of the sales process will be:

1. Getting an   _____
   Appointment
   _____

2. Opening   _____
   the Call
   _____

3. Discovering   _____
   Buyer Needs
   _____

4. Making a   _____
   Recommendation
   _____

5. Asking for   _____
   the Business
   _____

6. Installing and   _____
   Implementing
   _____

Index

Sales Versatility Training

The purpose of this book is to help you increase your sales effectiveness through versatility. Reading a book can be very helpful—we hope that this one has been so for you.

We also know that it is sometimes easier to learn and apply new concepts through other kinds of methods.

Therefore, in order to help you develop and enhance your sales versatility skills, we have created other programs in *The Versatile Salesperson* family for you to use:

- *Sales Strategy Computer Disk:* Designed for individuals to use in profiling buyers and developing selling strategies. Available in most popular personal business computer formats.
- *Core Seminar:* Designed for groups. Modular, one to two days. Based on your objectives, the seminar covers social style characteristics, style identification, sales versatility strategies, and actual skill practice in applying versatility to the six phases of the sale.
- *Follow-Up Modules.* Designed for groups, teachable by sales managers. Half-day in length. Helps develop sales versatility in four separate areas: Questioning and Listening, Answering Objections, Making Recommendations, and Closing to the Customer.

If you wish further information about these programs you may contact:

Sales & Marketing Effectiveness Curriculum
Wilson Learning Corporation
6950 Washington Avenue South
(612) 944-2880